Home of the Fleet

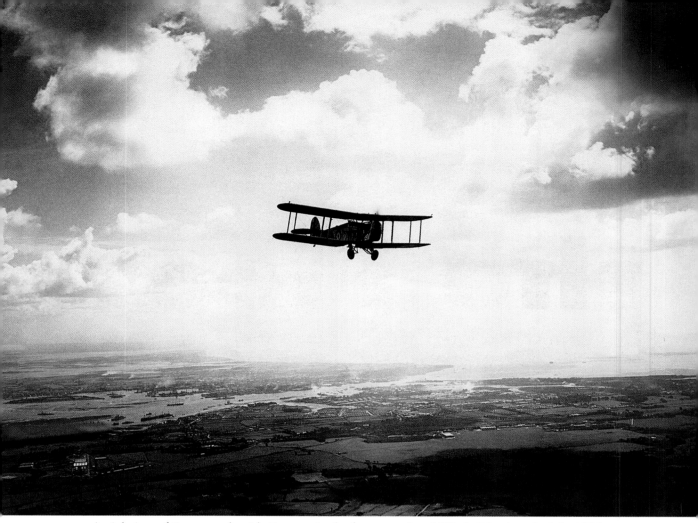

Aerial view of Portsmouth with Gosport in the foreground and Whale Island to the left, 1930s.

Home of the Fleet

A CENTURY OF PORTSMOUTH ROYAL DOCKYARD IN PHOTOGRAPHS

STEPHEN COURTNEY AND BRIAN PATTERSON

Royal Naval
MUSEUM
PUBLICATIONS

SUTTON PUBLISHING

First published in 2005 by
Sutton Publishing Limited · Phoenix Mill
Thrupp · Stroud · Gloucestershire · GL5 2BU
in association with the Royal Naval Museum, Portsmouth

British Library Cataloguing in Publication Data
A catalogue record for this book is available from the British Library

ISBN 0-7509-2285-0

Endpapers, front: View from the top of the 240-ton crane, 1944; *back*: Women sewing canvas patches on to a Berthron lifeboat.

Typeset in 11/14pt Sabon.
Typesetting and origination by
Sutton Publishing Limited.
Printed and bound in England by
J.H. Haynes & Co. Ltd, Sparkford.

This book is dedicated to the memory of
Dr Chris Howard Bailey
Oral Historian
of the
Royal Naval Museum

HMS *Drake* lying alongside South Railway Jetty. She was built at Pembroke Dockyard and completed for service in November 1903. She was recommissioned at Portsmouth in January 1905 as flagship of the Second Cruiser Squadron of the Atlantic Fleet, Rear Admiral HSH Prince Louis of Battenberg. She was torpedoed and sunk by U-79 off Rathlin Island, north of Ireland, on 2 October 1917.

CONTENTS

Portsmouth Harbour with armoured cruisers and pre-Dreadnought battleships filling the scene, *c.* 1910.

PREFACE AND ACKNOWLEDGEMENTS

*H*ome of the Fleet is intended to show the changes that have occurred in the old Royal Dockyard at Portsmouth over the last hundred years. It is not meant to be a complete history of the dockyard over that period for it is too big a subject for a picture book, which is exactly what *Home of the Fleet* is, a book of photographic images over the last one hundred years, broken into ten-year chapters. I have tried to add interest to each of the periods with a small account of the main events of the time. In some chapters not all the main events are covered for they are too numerous for the size of this work. On occasions I have taken the liberty of interpreting what the yardmen may have felt. Some may say I am wrong in doing this, but I entered the dockyard in 1952 and served until 1993, when I took early retirement and went to work for the Portsmouth Naval Base Property Trust in the Naval Base. At the time of writing I am still employed by that organisation. So for most of my life I have been in the dockyard; working, laughing and grumbling; often cold, wet, hungry and tired; at times fed up. The pulse of the dockyard matey has been my pulse.

One must always be mindful that the story of the dockyard is also the story of the development of the warship. The two cannot be divorced, nor can the story of the city of Portsmouth be separated from the dockyard. The city grew up around the dockyard and owes its very existence to it, and the dockyard is at Portsmouth because of its geographical location in relation to Europe and local shipbuilding resources. The city is in essence the people and it was the people who populated the dockyard.

In considering the history of the city of Portsmouth and its great institutions, such as the parks, libraries, esplanades and beaches, along with the fine Guildhall, it is well to consider that they might not have been built had it not been for the blood, sweat and tears of the dockyard men and the dockyard they served. Nor would there have been the need for the great works of fortification that surround the city, and which are so much a part of its history. In the heritage area of the dockyard the story of the great historic ships and the Royal Navy is displayed for the world to see and enjoy; but, regrettably, nowhere is the story of the dockyard told. An industry that was at one time the largest single industrial complex in the world, it was often in the forefront of industrial technology and today is the oldest naval base in the country with a history spanning 800 years.

The Portsmouth Royal Dockyard Historical Society was founded in 1982 with the hope of telling this story. In 1994 the society gave way to the Portsmouth Royal Dockyard Historical Trust which now pursues this aim. It is sincerely hoped that *Home of the Fleet* will prove both enjoyable and informative to the reader and enlighten those who have wondered what went on behind the dockyard walls.

The majority of the research material for the text of this book has come from the Dockyard Collection. Little of the collection is catalogued. In consequence, searching for material of specific periods of time has been almost impossible. It has been a case of trawling through odd bundles of signals, memos, orders and work books in the hope that something of interest would emerge. In the end the investigations usually raised more questions, which my shipwright training, although not essential for research, was often of great help in understanding. The Docking Register is a record of all dry-docking, undockings and slipping that took place in the yard's dry docks. I have found it to be a most useful source of reference in gauging the flow of work in the dockyard and it would make an excellent future publication for ship buffs. For material on the latter part of the century, I found the dockyard's own newspaper, *Trident*, from January 1969 to March 1994, of great value. For the early part of the century the city's own newspaper, the *Evening News*, was another valued source of reference, as were the City of Portsmouth Corpor-ation Records. Often it was the finding of an odd signal or memo that set me on the trail to a fascinating discovery. Regrettably, at times the discovery was outside the scope of the book and will have to wait another time for its telling. The silhouettes at the head of each chapter are from my own shaky hand and any errors are mine. All of the photographic images have come from the photographic collection of the Portsmouth Royal Dockyard Historical Trust and the photographic collection of the Royal Naval Museum at Portsmouth. To Stephen Courtney, the Curator of Photographs, go my thanks for his valued assistance with this work.

I would sincerely like to thank the publishers, Sutton Publishing, members of the Royal Naval Museum and the Portsmouth Naval Base Property Trust for the patience and kindness shown to me after the book was started in 1999, when in December of that year I was struck down with a stroke that left me paralysed on the left side of my body. (I am left-handed.) They did not give up the idea of my finishing this book even though I had, hence the long delay in its completion. A debt of gratitude is owed to the late Dr Chris Howard Bailey of the Royal Naval Museum, whose persistence in bullying me into finishing this work, is now greatly appreciated. I should also like to thank the Director of the Royal Naval Museum, Cambell McMurray, and Peter Goodship of the Portsmouth Naval Base Property Trust for their help and kindness in completing this work. Also to Lorraine Carpenter of the Property Trust go my thanks for her patience and valued help in the final drafting. I am indebted to Keith Thomas for reading the final draft of the book; he was Chief Executive, Royal Dockyards during the difficult period of the 1981 defence review and his comments were of great value. I should also like to thank Victoria Ingles, Lynn New, Jeannette Luczkawski, Archie Malley and members of the Dockyard Trust Support Group for their assistance. To everyone I am truly grateful.

Brian H. Patterson
'Olrig'
June 2005

The aircraft carrier HMS *Ark Royal* entering Portsmouth Harbour, 23 March 1988. She has been fitted with three Phalanx Close-in Weapons Systems as a result of lessons learnt in the 1982 Falklands conflict.

The first iron-hulled, sea-going, armoured battleship HMS *Warrior* of 1860 in Portsmouth, 1880s.

CHAPTER 1

THE VICTORIAN PERIOD, 1837–1900

No other period in naval history has seen such change in thinking and design of warships as the Victorian era. When the young Queen Victoria came to the throne in 1837 the British battle fleet still consisted of sail-of-the-line warships of the Trafalgar period. True, there were improvements in design, but to all outward appearances the wooden bulwarks of old England, manned by men with hearts of oak, seemed unchanged. The smooth-bore cannon still lorded the waters within its small and inaccurate range.

When the great queen died in 1901, the seeds of the Dreadnought battleship were germinating in the minds of men: engines capable of driving the ship through the water at 22 knots, electricity, the locomotive torpedo, wireless telegraphy, telescopic gunsights and rangefinders controlling guns that were able to throw an 850lb shell more than 10,000 yards. The submarine and torpedo boat were matters of concern for the far-seeing naval tactician. In these weapons they could see an end to the close blockade, the principal weapon for an island race against its European enemies. With weapons such as these in enemy hands, British squadrons would be prevented from sitting on the doorstep of an enemy port. Such was the change in sixty years.

To the British public in general it was 'sixty glorious years' of towns growing up around the artisan's dwelling place, of gardens, bathrooms and forecourted houses. Gas and electricity were revolutionising domestic living standards, while trains and trams unified distant parts of the country. London was now within one and a half hours' travelling time of Portsmouth by rail, a far cry from the days of the stagecoach. Towns boasted of their water and sewage treatment plants, their schools and lending libraries, their churches, and people's parks where the populace could walk on a Sunday afternoon. The seaside was accessible to the inland population of the country and a new development, the Victorian seaside pier, became a much-sought-after attraction. It was to Portsmouth, with its seaside resort of Southsea, that the populace came and paid their tuppence for a deckchair in which to sit on the beach, eating their winkles and whelks from rolled-up cones of newspaper, as they stared out across the historic waterway of Spithead, while the great ships of the world's most powerful navy rode at anchor, or steamed majestically in and out of Portsmouth Harbour past the seafront. They felt safe and secure behind this sure shield, with an immense pride that their country was the head of the greatest Empire the world had ever seen, one on which it could truly be said that the sun never set.

For the Royal Dockyard at Portsmouth it was sixty years of continuous change. Steam had revolutionised the dockyard, but it was the increase in the size of ships that made it grow in overall area. At the end of the Napoleonic Wars in 1815 Portsmouth boasted the world's first steam-operated dry-docking complex, comprising six stone dry docks surrounding the 'Great Stone Basin' (No. 1 Basin). These were all interconnected by underground culverts terminating at an underground reservoir, which was originally built as a wet dock. It was emptied by pumping into the harbour, using a Bolton and Watt steam engine, installed in 1798. Mobile steam pumps were introduced in 1803. Steam made possible the first mechanised wood mill and later the world's first mass-production factory for the manufacture of ships' pulley-blocks. There was also a highly mechanised copper mill. All this naturally increased the demand for fresh water and so its

Looking north up through Portsmouth Harbour, c. 1898. Although the wooden-walled ships are not named, it is known that *Victory*, *St Vincent* and *Wellington* were in the harbour at this time. *Marlborough* was in the dockyard, as were *Hannibal* and *Asia* as receiving ships. The *Ariadne* was joined by a bridge to the *Donegal* to form HMS *Vernon*. The original *Vernon* was renamed *Actaeon*. Other wooden-walls were the *Pitt* coal hulk, *Royal George*, receiving ship for the Royal Yacht, and the *Edgar*, built in 1859 as a 91-gun two-decker. She was the last wooden line-of-battleship to serve in the Channel Fleet. For many years she was a quarantine ship anchored off the Mother Bank.

The 1890s. Another view of the harbour, facing north. The white ships alongside the jetties are troopships. The harbour chain-ferry can be seen to the right of the picture.

extraction from wells was mechanised, using steam as the motive power. Naysmith demonstrated his steam hammer in 1832 at the dockyard smithery. Steam was also introduced for the testing of ships' anchors and chains in Stoney Lane in the dockyard. Despite all these changes the general size of the dockyard had hardly changed, but for a few acres.

The first Victorian expansion of the dockyard was brought about by the need to build, service and install steam machinery into ships of the fleet. The Steam Basin (No. 2 Basin), the surrounding dry docks and workshops were built between 1843 and 1848, with further buildings and docks being added over the next ten years.

When Queen Victoria opened the Steam Basin on 25 May 1848 it marked the final acknowledgement that steam was to be the prime motive power for the fleet in the foreseeable future. These new works confirmed the prestigious position the dockyard had held for many years as one of the largest industrial complexes in the world.

Who could have foreseen that within twelve years this great new steam complex would be rendered inadequate with the building of the iron battleships *Warrior* and *Black Prince*, the largest warships in the world? Portsmouth had only one dry dock that could accommodate these two new leviathans, No. 11 Dock, and this was still in the process of being built. A further dock could be gained if the caisson dividing Nos 7 and 10 Docks was removed. As these ships would become the rule for future naval construction and not the exception, then clearly a whole new complex of dry docks and basins would have to be built.

So it was that in 1864 the Lords of the Admiralty were granted the necessary parliamentary powers to enclose 180 acres of harbour mudlands and part of Portsea Island for the building of four basins, three dry docks and two locks, with the provision for a further two dry docks at a later date to accommodate a new fleet of Warrior-type warships. It is mainly this complex of docks that serves today as the Naval Base Repair Facility. From the building of the *Warrior* until the 1880s the Royal Navy was to see many strange types of warships added to the strength of the fleet. In common with other navies of the world of this period, fleets progressed from the broadside ship of the sailing era to the armoured-citadel type vessel, through to the muzzle-loading turret and on to the open-barbette battleship, finally emerging as the turbine-driven, all-big-gun battleship of the Dreadnought class.

It was many of these early types of ship that the First Sea Lord, Sir John Arbuthnot (Jacky) Fisher, referred to as 'too weak to fight and too slow to run away', in dealing with his great reforms of the Royal Navy. The policy of maintaining a fleet of twice the strength of the strongest European power ensured a steady naval building programme of which the dockyard at Portsmouth received a major share.

The introduction of the steam battleship also brought great fear to Britain, for now an invasion force could cross the Channel and land in a matter of hours. No longer would 'they' have to await favourable winds. This threat was eased slightly with the signing of the Franco-Prussian peace treaty, for it saw an end to the Bonaparte reign and the birth of the Third Republic. However, it also saw the unification of the South German states with the North German Confederation to form the German Empire. In January 1871 King William of Prussia was proclaimed the German Emperor at Versailles. Part of the treaty conditions was the splitting of the Alsace-Lorraine provinces, with their large iron- and coalfields, in Germany's favour. It was not long before Wilhelm, the German Kaiser, was to introduce and in time vigorously pursue a naval building policy that would be a direct challenge to the Royal Navy and the British Empire.

In 1903 Fisher became Commander-in-Chief at Portsmouth, the stepping stone to the First Sea Lord's position, which he was offered in May 1904. He insisted on taking office on 21 October, Trafalgar Day. Fisher had always stood for change, reform, efficiency and readiness. If war was to come to the Empire, as he believed it would, then he was determined to see a British fleet ready to 'hit first, hit hard and keep on hitting'. It was his vigorous reforms and building policy that were to culminate in a 'Grand Fleet' the like of which the world had never seen, nor would ever see again. Portsmouth's Royal Dockyard was destined to be the lead player in these great events, setting records which would be almost impossible to match even today as the great inter-national battleship-building race gained momentum and hurtled towards the first great world war.

The Royal Naval College in 1865. Built between 1729 and 1732, it was the Royal Naval Academy until 1806, then served as the Royal Naval College from 1808. The Royal Naval School of Navigation opened in 1906 and served until 1941, when the building was seriously damaged by German bombing. The school was evacuated to Southwick House and became known as HMS *Dryad*. The building to the left of the picture is thought to be the old military guardhouse.

Overlooking No. 2 Basin and on towards Fareham, *c.* 1899. In the bottom left-hand corner can be seen the tall 40-ton sheerlegs and, nearby, a chain dredger. No. 5 Slipway and the building sheds can be seen at the back of the long Steam Factory (1845). Two torpedo boats are moored at the entrance to No. 11 Dry Dock which also has torpedo boats in it, and nearby two boilers are being transported on railway trucks. A light cruiser is moored to the outer wall.

HMS *Iris* lying alongside Pitch House Jetty. *Iris* was a dispatch vessel (second-class cruiser) built at Pembroke Dockyard and completed in April 1879. She became a tender to HMS *St Vincent* at Portsmouth for mechanical training of boys in 1903–4 and was sold in 1905. In the background can be seen the wooden sheds covering Nos 3, 4 and 5 Docks. These were designed by Sir Robert Seppings in the late 1820s. They were remarkable structures in that the roofs were supported on rows of wooden pillars and the expanse of the roofs was supported on the principle of trussing with a complete absence of cross-beams. The sheerlegs were built in 1835–7 and were 142ft high. The date of the picture is thought to be around the 1890s.

The torpedo boat destroyer *Hasty* in the tidal basin of the dockyard, *c.* 1895. *Hasty* was built at Yarrow in 1894 at a cost of £36,000. She had a maximum speed of 27 knots and a crew of fifty-three. She was sold in 1912.

The Dockyard Main Gate at the Hard, *c.* 1900. When the gate was widened in 1943 the wicket gate on the left-hand side, along with the gas jet pipe-lighter for dockyard men to light their clay pipes, was lost. Note the wooden boathouses on the left just inside the gate. They are said to date from the 1690s. They were demolished in 1939 to make way for the building of No. 4 Boathouse. On the right can be seen the dockyard muster bell.

Opposite, above: The dockyard as it was in 1898 before the building of C and D Locks. In the foreground is No. 9 Dry Dock followed by A and B Locks. Just above them is Fitting Out Basin No. 3 and to the right is Rigging Basin No. 4, with Repairing Basin No. 5 in the bottom right-hand corner. The Fitting Out Basin became the present day C and D Locks. The promontory dividing the Rigging Basin and Repair Basin was demolished to form one large basin, apart from a small section on the eastern side which is the promontory in No. 3 Basin today. Note the signal station on top of the Main Pumping Station in the bottom right-hand corner.

Opposite: The old Marlborough Gate in 1898. The original dockyard wall of 1711 and the police building on the left of the picture are still there today, but the little houses, pubs and shops have long since disappeared, mainly as a result of German bombing in the Second World War. The land was taken over by the yard in 1944. In the dockyard this area was known as the Marlborough salient because it almost cut the yard in half. Its absorption within the dockyard boundary was blamed on the German bombing, but it had been planned in the 1920s and 30s.

Following spread: The old and the new of the Dockyard Fire Brigade. The new motor engine is a Merryweather, proudly displayed alongside the traditional horse-drawn pumping engine. The minimal harness on the horse could only be used on very flat ground such as in the dockyard. The picture is taken outside the Admiral Superintendent's residence at the end of Long Row in the Parade.

CHAPTER 2

THE DREADNOUGHTS 1900–10

On 27 April 1876 Princess Louise opened the second great Victorian extension of the dockyard, which was made necessary by the increased length of the Warrior-class battle fleet. On that day she also launched HMS *Inflexible*, the first of the great Portsmouth-built armoured battleships. The walls of her armoured citadel were 24 inches thick, the thickest ever mounted in a ship. She was also the first ship to be launched and lit by electricity. It is said she had the dubious honour of being the first in which a sailor was killed by electrocution. For the next thirty years battleship design took on some very odd shapes. Often the seeds of the modern battleship seemed to germinate only to wither on the vine of an industry not technically capable of producing the materials required.

During this period man's ingenuity was often dogged by the puzzle of what form a modern naval battle would take, what range it would be fought at or what would be the best-calibre gun or the highest speed for the best coal consumption. All these matters tended to cloud the illusion of the perfect battleship. For a maritime nation such as Great Britain, whose life depended on dominance of the world's sea lanes, these were perplexing issues. In competition with other sea-minded nations, the country entered a race that with the best endeavour could not be won: a race of guns versus armour. A bigger gun demanded thicker armour; thicker armour demanded a bigger gun to defeat it. In the end a battleship tended to be a compromise based on the material and finance available at the time of her building.

In 1904 Sir John Fisher, Britain's First Sea Lord, had all the pieces in place to produce a revolutionary, all-big-gunned battleship: the industrial base of Britain, with its huge iron and shipbuilding industries; the turbine, developed by Parsons, which would revolutionise ships' engine rooms and give him his superior speed; an ordnance industry capable of producing large-calibre guns; and a team of exceptionally talented men to bring the dream into reality. Fisher summed up the destructive power of the new ship with 'once the range had been obtained, a 12 inch gun would fire one aimed shot every minute. Six guns would allow a deliberately aimed shell with a huge bursting charge every 10 seconds, 50 percent of these should be hits at 6,000 yards. Three 12 inch shells

The pre-Dreadnought *Britannia* seen here prior to her launch on 10 December 1904 by Lady Londonderry. *Britannia* was one of eight King Edward-class battleships. The battleship *New Zealand* of this class was launched at Portsmouth on 4 February 1904. She later changed her name to *Zealandia*. The *Britannia* had the distinction of being the last major warship to be sunk in the First World War. She was struck by two torpedoes from the German submarine UB-50 off Cape Trafalgar on 9 November 1918, two days before the Armistice. She remained afloat for 3½ hours before sinking.

bursting on board every minute would be hell!' Such was the dream.

Portsmouth Dockyard was chosen to build the new vessel. Since it was an enclosed government establishment, security and control of the project could be more easily achieved and this would be essential, for it was a mighty but necessary gamble and time was the enemy. Britain had maintained a system that expressed its maritime power in terms of numbers of capital ships compared with its nearest European rival. The new revolutionary warship would render all other battleships obsolete. If other major industrial nations realised what the British were doing, they would quickly follow in their wake, and if they could achieve a quicker building pace then supremacy of the seas would slip from Britain's grasp. The well-being of the Empire and the liberty of Britons would be at stake. The true merits of the new battleship would have to be concealed until after the conclusion of her trials. Speed of building was to be the very essence.

The first keel plates were laid at No. 5 Slipway on Monday 2 October 1905. By 25 November the main deck-beams were being erected. On 10 February, just four months after the laying of her keel plates, she was launched with a bottle of Australian wine by King Edward VII, watched by a jubilant Fisher. The speed of building was unprecedented and is still a record for an armoured ship. All the boilers were in place and over 2,000 tons of armour erected by 6 March. In June her turbines were installed, along with six of her big 12in guns. July saw the installation of the other four 12in guns and by August

her displacement had risen to 15,380 tons. In October, a year and a day after her laying-down the *Dreadnought* went to sea for trials. On 11 December 1906 HMS *Dreadnought* was commissioned into the Royal Navy. Previously, average building times for battleships of the Royal Navy had been thirty-three months.

In was an impressive achievement and the rest of the world looked on in wonderment. The London *Times* correspondent in Washington reported, 'That such a ship could have been built so quickly and so secretly astonishes naval experts.' Many believed her building was a direct result of lessons learnt in the recent Russo-Japanese war, where it was known that Japan had allowed Royal

A week before the *Dreadnought*'s launch on 10 February by King Edward VII and 123 days after the laying of the first keel plate. On the day of a launch schools closed and shops shut early as thousands of people flocked into the dockyard, where military bands would entertain the crowds with popular airs while waiting for the dignitaries to arrive. It was not uncommon for crowds of 50,000–60,000 to attend the launchings of the great battleships. The town had great pride in the dockyard and its achievements, whence its wealth came!

The *Dreadnought* fitting out in No. 15 Dock. A year and a day from the laying of her keel, *Dreadnought* steamed out of the harbour for trials. The speed of her building still stands today as a record for an armoured battleship and her conception set the standard for future battleship construction and design. When the world learned of her, all older battleships became known as pre-Dreadnoughts and those that came after her bore the classification of Dreadnought.

Navy observers on board Admiral Togo's fleet. A close relationship had developed between Japan and Britain, and especially between the Royal Navy and the fledgling Imperial Japanese Navy, which many other nations viewed with mistrust. But to the people of Portsmouth it was a matter of great pride in their dockyard and in the people who worked there, for they knew that the eyes of the world were on them and that the world was asking, 'How did they do it?'

It was estimated that the speed of building the *Dreadnought* gave Britain about a three-year lead. To achieve such a building pace required a highly skilled craftsman-based industry and demanded huge expenditure of overtime. At times the average working day was eleven and a half hours long, six days a week. Of the 8,000 men in the yard at that time, nearly 3,000 were involved in the work on the *Dreadnought* at peak periods, and the men knew that if the ship was successful other orders would follow.

In the ships that followed *Dreadnought*, Portsmouth built the lead ship of all the Admiralty-planned battleship classes, a statement of the high regard the Admiralty had for the expertise in the dockyard at that time. Between 1904 and 1915 nine Dreadnought battleships were

HMS *Dreadnought* being warped into No. 15 Dock for repairs. On the left of the picture can be seen the Dreadnought battleship *Bellerophon* fitting out. She was launched on 27 July 1907 and completed in February 1909. At this time the Dreadnought battleship *St Vincent* was building on No. 5 Slipway before her launch on 10 September 1908.

built in the dockyard on the same slipway, No. 5. The *Dreadnought* was the smallest of all the Dreadnoughts, being a mere 21,845 tons when fully loaded. But at the time of her building she was the largest battleship afloat. In building her, Portsmouth Dockyard was faced with an age-old problem. Only one dry dock, No. 15, could safely accommodate her 82ft beam. More importantly, the locks used as canals to move ships from the harbour to the inner repair basins, and whose entrances were also 82ft wide, could no longer be used for this purpose. Only the entrance to the Rigging Basin in Fountain Lake at the north end of the dockyard could be used (this entrance was closed in May 1923). Unfortunately the depth of water over the entrance sill restricted movement to only fourteen times a year. Lord Charles Beresford, then Parliamentary Representative for Portsmouth, was told by Mr McKenna, First Lord of the Admiralty, that when the *Dreadnought* was fully loaded at her deep draught, she could only pass through the Fountain Lake jetty entrance on three days a year. Clearly something would have to be done and done quickly.

By the end of 1906 plans were being prepared for new docks in Portsmouth Dockyard that would give a length, with their caisson in the outer stops, of 921ft 6in. These were eventually to materialise as the present-day C and D Locks. The walls dividing the Victorian extension basins would be removed to form one large inner basin, now known as No. 3 Basin. The east–west centre wall of the basin was

The launching of the *Bellerophon* on 27 July 1907. Princess Henry of Battenburg takes the mallet, made from *Victory* oak, from the launching casket, which also contains a chisel. She is then assisted in cutting the rope that can be seen going around the stern. Two long, heavy weights are suspended from the rope, which then fall and knock the last retaining shore away, releasing the ship from her building-berth. On the left of the picture, in front of the man with his hands behind his back, can be seen the 'creep pointer', which shows if the ship is moving. The charming lady on the right of the photograph is Charlotte, the wife of Mr Pescott Frost, Secretary to the Admiral and founder of the original Dockyard Museum.

A moment frozen in time on a glass-plate negative: the keel-laying ceremony of the battleship *St Vincent* on No. 5 Slipway on 30 December 1907. *St Vincent* was launched on 10 September 1908 by the Countess of Beauchamp and commissioned on 3 May 1910. She served throughout the First World War and fought at the Battle of Jutland. She was discarded under the terms of the Washington Treaty on 1 December 1921 and broken up at Dover the following year.

reduced to half its length to form a promontory on which was built a large hammer-head crane with a lifting capacity of 250 tons. The hammer-head crane was so-called because the jib was shaped like the metal head of a claw hammer seen in profile. It was to dominate the Portsmouth skyline for seventy-three years. No. 14 Dry Dock would be rebuilt to a larger format. A new machine shop known as the MED Factory, one of the largest machine shops in England, was also opened at this time specifically for the Dreadnought-building programme.

When the Dreadnought-building period finally ended in 1920, thirty-five battleships and thirteen battlecruisers had been built at a cost of some £151,000,000, and in the design stages were battleships of 48,500 tons standard displacement armed with nine 18in guns, and similar battlecruisers. It had been a momentous period in the naval and shipbuilding history of the world, the like of which will never be seen again. The much-published destructive power of the Dreadnoughts at the beginning of the First World War generated dreams of a new Trafalgar, but at the end of four bitter years of war the dreams had failed to become reality. As for the *Dreadnought* herself, she had the distinction of being the only battleship to ram and sink a German U-boat, the U-29, on 18 March 1915. After a short life she was sold in 1922 for £44,000 and broken up.

Shipwrights knocking out the last of the keel blocks at the bow end of the Dreadnought battleship *King George V*, 7 October 1911. The ship is built on these keel or building blocks. Prior to the launch the ship's weight has to be transferred from the building block to the sliding ways while she sits in the cradle, and the building blocks are then removed.

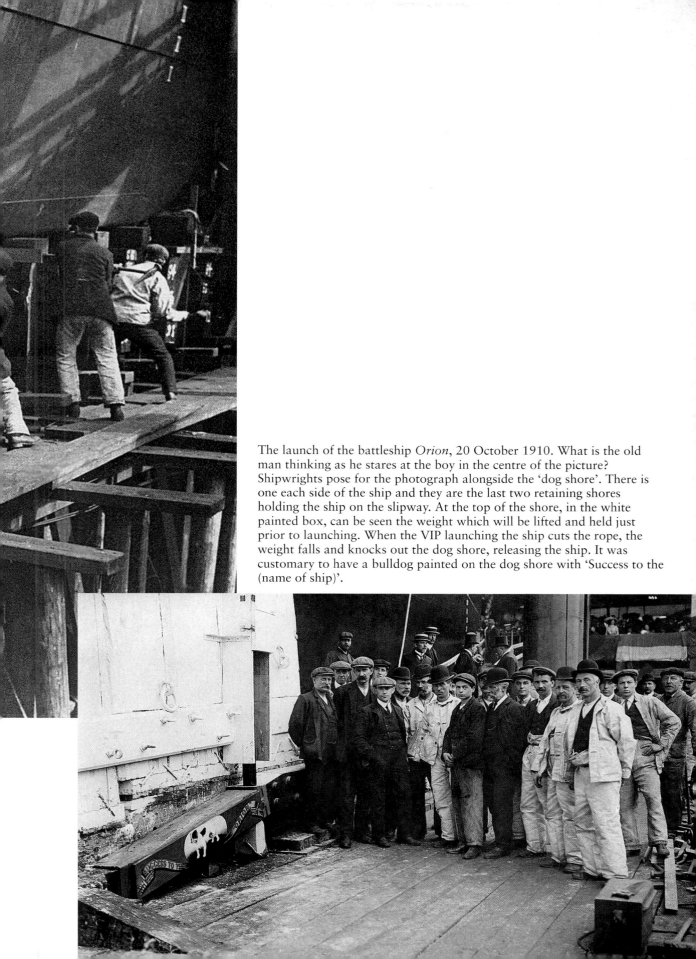

The launch of the battleship *Orion*, 20 October 1910. What is the old man thinking as he stares at the boy in the centre of the picture? Shipwrights pose for the photograph alongside the 'dog shore'. There is one each side of the ship and they are the last two retaining shores holding the ship on the slipway. At the top of the shore, in the white painted box, can be seen the weight which will be lifted and held just prior to launching. When the VIP launching the ship cuts the rope, the weight falls and knocks out the dog shore, releasing the ship. It was customary to have a bulldog painted on the dog shore with 'Success to the (name of ship)'.

The launch of the battleship *Iron Duke*, 12 October 1912. Three anchors have been dropped, bringing the ship to rest in the harbour to await the dockyard tugs. Meanwhile dockyard men collect the floating grease and timber packing from the slipway to reuse at the next launch.

Alberta was a Royal Yacht built at Pembroke in 1863. She was a two-funnelled paddle-wheel vessel with three masts and acted as a tender to the main Royal Yacht *Victoria and Albert II*. She became a great favourite with Queen Victoria. *Alberta* was paid off on 30 March 1912 and broken up in the dockyard in 1913.

CHAPTER 3

THE FIRST WORLD WAR PERIOD, 1910–20

To test the efficiency of the naval reserve system, a mobilisation of the reserve fleet was ordered for July 1914, and was to be combined with a fleet review. This entailed much work for the Royal Dockyards, which were already at near capacity with the effects of the naval building programme. On 16 July there assembled at Spithead a vast armada of 24 Dreadnoughts, 35 pre-Dreadnoughts, 18 armoured cruisers, 31 light cruisers, 78 destroyers, and smaller vessels and submarines; in all, forty miles of ships were drawn up in twelve long lines. A total of 648 vessels was assembled for the review and it was an unprecedented spectacle. Sixteen seaplanes flew over the Royal Yacht in formation almost as an omen of things to come. The fleet dispersed on 20 July by steaming in single file past the King in his yacht anchored off the Nab Tower, each ship dipping her ensign as she passed him. It must have been a sombre spectacle, and for many a last salute. On 29 July the fleet, now named the Grand Fleet, left Portland in secrecy for its wartime base at Scapa Flow in the Orkney Islands.

When war was declared at 11 p.m. on 4 August 1914, the programme of work for Portsmouth Dockyard for 1913–14

showed the battleship *Iron Duke* completing, the *Queen Elizabeth* building and the preparatory work well advanced on the *Royal Sovereign*. The programme of work goes on to name 17 battleships and battlecruisers, 82 cruiser-type heavy ships, 37 destroyers, 17 submarines and 11 dockyard craft. Parts of the dockyard were still in the process of being rebuilt in consequence of the Dreadnought programme. C Lock was opened on 8 April 1913 for the docking of the battlecruiser *Princess Royal*; the opening of D Lock was not until March 1914. No. 14 Dry Dock, which had been closed for lengthening and widening of the caisson entrance, was opened on 9 November 1914 with the dry-docking of the battleship *Hindustan*.

The main coaling point for the fleet in the dockyard was on the north-west side of the tidal basin and served by ten 1-ton hydraulic cranes and two 10-ton tips for rapid loading of vessels. This facility was displaced by the building of the new locks, and coaling had to be done from colliers and hulks moored in the harbour. During 1912 an oil fuel depot was established on the Gosport side of the harbour with the building of huge oil tanks. Ships requiring refuelling were placed alongside the oiling pier and fuel oil pumped into the ships' tanks through pipes, a far cleaner and less laborious procedure than that of coaling ships.

The day before war was declared the local paper, the *Evening News*, published a notice from the Commander-in-Chief Admiral Sir Hedworth Meux, instructing vessels entering or leaving harbour how to proceed. No vessel was to enter the harbour without permission or examination by an officer stationed off the west end of the Isle of Wight. The Needles passage was to be closed. No vessel was to approach a man-of-war or naval establishment. No vessel was allowed in without a special pilot and none could leave without permission. No movement would be allowed during fog or at night, when the boom across the harbour was in place. Patrols were quickly established in the Channel approaches to the harbour. It was strongly believed that if the German High Seas Fleet broke through the Royal Navy cordon and entered the Channel, Portsmouth would be its first objective. These fears were further intensified on 16 December, when German warships bombarded Scarborough, Whitby and Hartlepool. Long-established military fortifications around the Spithead anchorage and dockyard were

A fine aerial view of HMS *Dolphin* probably taken during or just after the First World War. The fort passed from the War Department to the Admiralty in 1904, when it was developed into the Royal Navy's first submarine base. The two vessels lying at the harbour mouth are boom tenders. The boom can be seen on the shore side of each vessel.

Fountain Lake Jetty, at one time known as Asia Pontoon, after the wooden-walled ship *Asia*, which was moored there for many years. The Round Tower on the left-hand side was part of Frederick's Battery, built in 1845, which ran across the north-eastern corner, where No. 2 Basin is today. During the 1860s' Great Extension it was taken down and rebuilt in its present position.

manned and their armaments put into a high state of readiness. At its peak, 50,000 troops were in the town's vicinity and at no time did the number fall below 25,000 men.

On 29 April 1915 the battleship *Royal Sovereign* was launched without ceremony or the vast crowds of spectators that were so familiar on these occasions. She was to be the last major warship built in the dockyard during the war, for repairs, conversions and dry-docking of warships were now the main themes of the yard. The submarines J 1, J 2, K 1, K 2 and K 5 were built in No. 13 Dry Dock and were the first submarines to be built in the dockyard. The K-class submarines were themselves a revolution, being the first steam-driven fleet submarines and capable of 24 knots.

The transport work, which included the shipment to France of tanks, locomotives, siege batteries, lorries, guns, ammunition and men, necessitated the appointment of a transport officer and staff under the direction of the Admiral Superintendent. The salvage of damaged vessels and the laying of additional moorings also involved a good deal of work for the dockyard. The naval stores system of the yard expanded with the growth of the fleet and the dockyard's workload. It was said to have 20,000 different items in stock at any time. The value of stores dealt with during 1917–18 reached a staggering £23 million. The manufacture of 12-pounder and 4in guns and shells, also undertaken in the yard during the war, added to the burden on the stores system. The introduction of motor lorries, which gradually replaced horse-drawn transport, did much to speed up the distribution of stores. Heavy loads such as steel plates, armour, ordnance, coal and timber, etc. used the dockyard railway system, which was worked by locomotives and the necessary rolling stock, and had over 20 miles of track connected by two lines to the mainline network. The annual dockyard consumption of coal before the war was running at 15,000 tons. With the many thousands of tons of steel plate, stores and timber required for building and refit work of the fleet it became clear that the dockyard railway system was the vital artery that kept the yard alive.

When the War Office issued its now famous poster 'Your King and Country need you', men in their thousands across the country flocked to join the colours. With the already published call for reservists to report for service the ranks of the dockyard started to thin. The situation was aggravated on 1 September 1914, when the Mayor of Portsmouth sent a telegram to the Secretary of State for War, offering to raise a battalion for Kitchener's Army. In under a year Portsmouth raised three battalions of 1,100 men each, for service with the Hampshire Regiment. The King conferred a knighthood upon the Mayor, Mr J.H. Corke, for his splendid work in this event. But for the hard-pressed dockyard with its rising workload of war-worn or damaged ships it was a constant drain of highly skilled manpower. In effect the dockyard was rapidly running out of its lifeblood.

Women had long been employed in the Colour Loft of the dockyard, making flags, and in selected clerical posts but they were few in number. There was no dockyard regulation for the employment of women outside these areas. But as the first dispatches from the sea and land wars were printed, showing the names of the fallen, and the train-loads of wounded began to arrive home, there stirred in women a patriotic flame that would be impossible to extinguish. In truth a desperate industry welcomed them but was sceptical as to what they could accomplish with their limited strength and skill.

The entry of women into the dockyard produced unseen benefits in allowing unskilled men to be trained and to move into semi-skilled positions. It was found that women could perform semi-skilled tasks as competently as men. Certain craft jobs were broken down into simple modules, allowing women to assist craftsmen in often-complicated tasks. The increased use of pneumatic hand tools and the increasing mechanisation of workshops compensated for the women's lack of skill in trades that often took a male apprentice seven years to learn, and in many areas more than made up for the women's lack of physical strength. With the closer integration of women into the male working environment, the practice of forcing women to enter the dockyard 15 minutes after men in the morning and leave before men at out-muster times soon became a great inconvenience to the working day and was abolished. Its demise did much to unify the workforce. Some 1,800 women were employed in the dockyard during the war, serving alongside men in every workshop, in the bottoms of dry docks, in timber yards, factories, foundries and the scrap grounds. Wherever they served they earned the respect of their fellow workmen and the gratitude of the nation as a whole. But even the influx of women could not make up for the loss of skilled craftsmen. The gap was partly filled by volunteers from Australia and Canada, serving in the dockyard for the duration of the war. They were known by their country of origin followed by the words 'Volunteer War Worker', an official category of workman applied by the dockyard.

At 11 p.m. on the night of 16 September 1916 the town and dockyard had a

Beatrice Hobbs was among the first female workers to be employed by the dockyard. She began work in the blockmills, and was later to say, 'We were given brand new brown-coloured overalls and a brass triangular badge that said we were on war service. We were so proud that we all went out into Queen St during the dinner hour and had a group photograph taken of us in our new overalls.' (*Beattie Hobbs*)

portent of the future. A German Zeppelin appeared in the night sky. The townspeople were aghast as they saw it held in the rays of searchlights. The shore batteries opened fire but only the smaller-calibre guns had the elevation to engage it, although not the range to reach it. It dropped four bombs before passing up the harbour. One narrowly missed HMS *Victory* moored in the harbour; others dropped close to the battlecruiser HMS *Renown*, which was in dry dock.

The increased size of the Royal Navy threw unprecedented demands on to the dockyard and its supporting establishments. Many of the yard's departments did not have the reserve space to grow. The age-old remedy of reclaiming land from the harbour to allow the dockyard to expand northwards was now impossible, with the gunnery establishment on Whale Island blocking its path.

Expansion eastwards into the town would displace hundreds of the dockyard's own workers and was clearly unacceptable. As the workforce climbed to over 25,000, relief was gained by the use of outstations, buildings taken over from the corporation, private industry and other War Department establishments. The increased use of electric motors, telephones, searchlights, etc. soon caused an embryo Electrical Department to rival the Construction and Engineering Departments of the dockyard as one of the prime movers. The Dockyard Generating Station, which had been built in 1904–6, was supplemented by two independent generating stations, and by 1918 all buildings and workshops were lit by electricity, with practically all workshop machinery being driven by electrical power.

With the expansion of naval bases and anchorages around the world, the problem of manning the dockyard became steadily more acute, for it was seen as a ready source of expertise to be tapped by the Admiralty. In consequence selected men were sent to other dockyards and bases in the Empire. On 6 April 1917 the first keel plates of the *Effingham*, a new cruiser, were laid down on No. 5 slipway. With the coming of peace, work on her stopped and she was to spend over four years on the slipway. In Parliament she was sarcastically referred to as HMS 'Methuselah'. She was finally launched on 8 June 1921 by the Marchioness of Salisbury and completed for service on 9 July 1925.

The war ended in the forest of Compiègne with the signing of the Armistice on 11 November 1918. The total of British dead was 947,000, of which 745,000 were from

To meet the requirements of larger battleships and battlecruisers, two new locks were built at the northern end of the dockyard. C Lock was opened on 8 April 1913, when the battlecruiser *Princess Royal* was admitted for dry-docking. D Lock was opened in April 1914, when the battlecruiser *Queen Mary* was dry-docked. The picture shows the *Queen Mary* in D Lock on 24 April and there appears to be work still going on to finish surfacing in the western caisson area.

No. 14 Dock, opened in 1896, was enlarged and reopened in November 1914. In the background can be seen the battleship *Queen Elizabeth* fitting out. She was the lead ship of her class and the largest battleship in the world to date. She is lying under the newly finished 240-ton hammer-head crane, which was also one of the largest in the world. Also in the picture are the 150-ton sheerlegs between Nos 14 and 15 Docks, which were at that time the highest sheerlegs in the country. The dock is being prepared by shipwrights for its reopening with the docking of the battleship *Hindustan* on 9 November 1914.

the United Kingdom. The signing was followed by rejoicing, tinged with melancholy as people's thoughts went back to the summer of 1914 before the war, when many saw their loved ones and friends for the last time. It seemed like the twilight of an era, as indeed it was. In that bleak winter of 1918 with its food shortages, the future seemed fearful with the knowledge that things would never be quite the same again.

In March of 1919 the manager of the Construction Department of the dockyard revealed part of the startling war record of the yard. From the commencement of war until the signing of the Armistice, 1,200 vessels had been refitted in the dockyard, including 40 battleships and battle-cruisers, 25 cruisers, over 400 destroyers, 150 torpedo boats, 140 trawlers and drifters, and 20 submarines and other vessels. During the same period, 1,658 war vessels were dry-docked or hauled up slipways for repair. The Naval War Memorial, when unveiled by the Duke of York at Southsea Common on 15 October 1924, bore 9,729 names from the Portsmouth command and 21 civilian employees. The town's war memorial was unveiled by the Duke of Connaught on 19 October 1921 and bore 5,000 names. The winning of peace had demanded a heavy price, of which Portsmouth and its dockyard had paid no small share.

A collapsible Berthron lifeboat being repaired in one of the boathouses. These boats were made of canvas with wooden stringers, and could be folded flat, much like an umbrella. (At one time they were called 'umbrella boats'.) The women workers are sewing canvas patches on the boat.

Opposite, above: In this view of 1913, the old caisson of No. 14 Dock is being dismantled and the steps each side are being cut back to give a new entrance width of 100ft. In the bottom corners of the picture can be seen the remains of the dock-bottom steps which were also cut back to allow ships with a wide bilge form to use the dock.

Opposite: On Saturday 20 December 1913 a serious fire broke out in the Sail Loft which quickly spread, engulfing the whole building and Semaphore Tower. Three men were on duty in the tower at the time, two of whom unfortunately perished in the flames. The picture shows the still-smoking ruins of the building.

The battlecruiser *Queen Mary* dry-docked in No. 14 Dock on 19 January 1915. The *Queen Mary* was sunk at the Battle of Jutland on 31 May 1916 with the loss of 1,266 of her crew. Jutland was to cause, and still continues to cause, controversy over who actually won. The public mood was eventually caught by this poem:

The Germans cry aloud, 'We've won!'   That those are the conquerors who run
But surely 'tis a curious view   And those the vanquished who pursue.

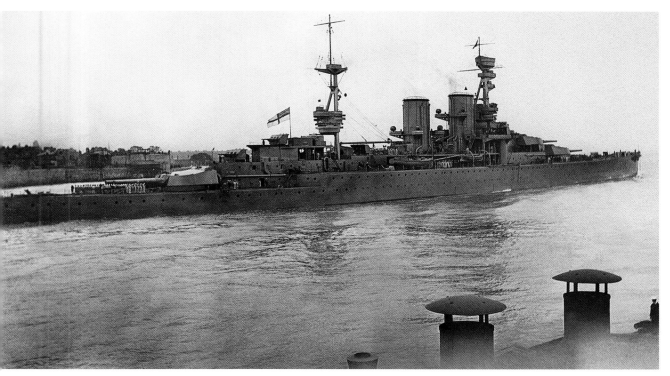

The battlecruiser *Renown* seen leaving Portsmouth, possibly after her April–July refit in 1919. The picture is taken from Fort Blockhouse, the submarine base that became known as HMS *Dolphin*.

Below: The dockyard-built, steam-driven submarine K 5 is seen in No. 2 Basin in 1917. The three-funnelled destroyer is HMS *Swift*. K 5 was exercising with the Atlantic Fleet west of the Scilly Islands on 20 January 1921. She was last seen at 11.44 hours, diving normally. Although wreckage was found, K 5 and her brave crew of fifty-seven were never seen again.

CHAPTER 4

THE BATTLESHIP HOLIDAY, 1920–30

The First World War was officially brought to an end with the signing of the Treaty of Versailles on Saturday 28 June 1919. The people celebrated in their own way and the Royal Navy marked the day by firing a 101-gun salute. The main celebrations were to be held on 19 July, when the town, the dockyard and the people had had time to prepare for the event. All the great gateways of the dockyard were decorated with the slogan 'Peace our Reward'.

The much-feared German High Seas Fleet had surrendered on 21 November 1918 and when they met the British Grand Fleet along with other Allied ships in the North Sea it was a sombre yet impressive occasion. The second-most-powerful navy in the world, the once proud High Seas Fleet, lay imprisoned in the cold waters of Scapa Flow under the watchful eye of the Royal Navy. On 21 June 1919, before the signing of the Versailles Treaty, Admiral von Reuter ordered the signal to be hoisted that was to scuttle seventy warships of the High Seas Fleet.

After this extraordinary event the Royal Navy found itself in the position of having over half of the world's effective fighting ships in nearly all classes. In 1919 the strength of the fleet stood at 61 battleships, 9 battlecruisers, 4 aircraft carriers, 30 cruisers, 90 light cruisers, 23 flotilla leaders, 432 destroyers, 147 submarines and thousands of smaller vessels, with many more major warships on slipways in the process of building. The manpower of the navy was close to half a million officers and men, who were well trained and hardened to battle after four long, weary years. It could truly be said that Britannia ruled the waves.

But Britain had been exhausted by the war. Much of her industrial power had been solely devoted to the production of war materials. This great war machine would have to be slowed and finally stopped. Prosperity and political stability depended on a quick return of industrial efficiency for improving the country's export trade. It became essential to cut government spending and by far the biggest budget in the government purse was defence. On 15 August 1919 the government approved the 'Ten-year Rule', a policy not abandoned until 1933, which instructed the services to cast their future estimates on the assumption that there would not be a war within ten years. In the civilian shipyards, warships planned or on the slipways in the course of

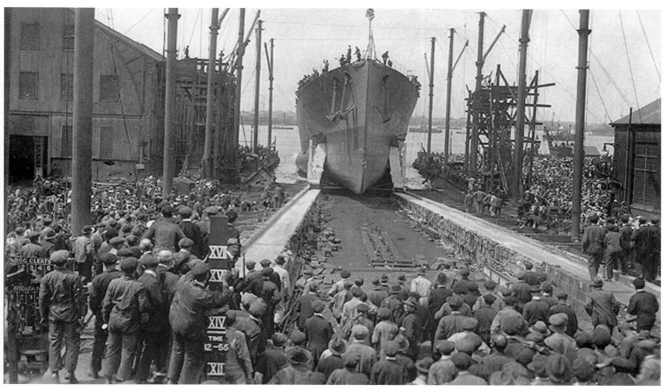

It appears to be a sunny day as the cruiser *Effingham* takes to the water on 8 June 1921. *Effingham* was laid down on 6 April 1917, but work was slowed and at times stopped as the need for large ocean-patrol cruisers had eased at that stage of the war. She was eventually completed on 2 July 1925. *Effingham* struck a rock off Narvik on 18 May 1940 and became a total loss. She was later destroyed by gunfire from British ships on 21 May 1940.

construction were cancelled and broken up. In some cases newly built ships in the process of fitting-out were towed to Royal Dockyards for completion. The D-class cruisers *Diomede*, *Despatch* and *Durban* went to Portsmouth, Chatham and Devonport respectively. This cut expenditure on new naval construction but, more importantly, it freed commercial slipways for a bigger merchant ship building programme. The British merchant fleet had been left much diminished and war-ravaged by a four-year confrontation at sea and its early recovery would be vital to an improvement in the economic situation.

In 1918 there were 23,000 people employed in the dockyard and with the announcement of peace many feared the expected discharges. The first steps on the road to peace would inevitably be redundancies, the first of which came in 1919. With men returning from the services and discharges from the dockyard, unemployment brought much suffering to the townspeople of Portsmouth, and with it often came confusion, for it was a complicated affair. The promise of a 'return to work' for those conscripted and reservists recalled to the colours had to be honoured. Women workers and men called in from other areas and occupations would have to be released. The volunteers who came from all parts of the Empire to serve in the dockyard would have to be sent home. Pensioners and time-expired men would also have to be released. Highly skilled established workers who had been sent to other dockyards and bases around the world would now be coming home and places in the dockyard would have to be found for them.

It was a complicated affair of 'hire, fire or transfer', which no doubt caused much anguish. To ease the growing distress in the town, the council undertook some civic works in the form of road building and improving the 3-mile stretch of esplanade by the Royal Marines' barracks at Eastney, all with the aid of government grants. Sir Herbert Cayzer, MP for the Portsmouth South Division, arranged for steamers from the Clan shipping line to be refitted in the dockyard in an effort to ease the discharges. Sir Thomas Fisher, a former naval officer, also helped employment in the dockyard when, as Superintendent of the Canadian Pacific Steamship Company, he arranged for the Atlantic liners to be refitted there. The dockyard craftsmen were given high praise by both companies for the excellent quality of their workmanship and the rapidity with which it was performed. Unfortunately the work came to an end at the close of 1923. When the Admiralty's request to the dockyards to consent to shorter working hours was rejected by the men (in Portsmouth and elsewhere), they ordered a reduction of the working week by seven hours and used the saving to re-enter 1,000 discharged men.

In 1913 Sir W.G. Armstrong Whitworth & Co. of Newcastle-upon-Tyne laid down the battleship *Almirante Cochrane* for the Chilean government, but work was suspended at the outbreak of war in 1914. Her sister ship the *Almirante Latorre* was much further advanced in her building and was completed for the Royal Navy as HMS *Canada*. She served throughout the war, being returned to Chile at the end of hostilities. In the later part of the war it was decided to complete the suspended battleship as an aircraft carrier for the Royal Navy. Her purchase was negotiated with the Chilean government and she was renamed HMS *Eagle* at her launch on 8 June

The battleship *Queen Elizabeth* and aircraft carrier *Eagle* exercising in the Channel. This picture is thought to date from 1923–4.

1918. She was partially completed for trials and left the Tyne under her own power for Portsmouth on 24 April 1920. At this stage she had only one funnel, a temporary mast, no armament and an incomplete island structure. After flying trials in the English Channel, which were to evaluate the starboard-island design, she was taken in hand at Portsmouth for modifications and completion of building work on 21 February 1921 and completed for full sea trials in September of 1923. It could be said she was the first of the true aircraft carriers as we know them today.

The effect of the Washington Treaty, drawn up by the world's major powers in 1922, was to restrict the size and growth of naval armaments. It was a major turning point in the history of the Royal Navy for, without contest and for the reason of economy, it accepted parity with the numerically inferior navy of the United States of America. Most of the signatories to the treaty found that in many classes of ships, they were not yet up to the limits imposed by the treaty and

consequently were in a position to build new ships. The Royal Navy, conversely, found that in many areas it was over the treaty limit and hence was forced to scrap ships that were but a few years old. There were probably as many advantages as disadvantages to the treaty but on the whole it did stop a return to a 'battleship race' between the nations of the world.

One of the clauses of the treaty was the 10,000-tons standard displacement cruiser, later to be known as the 'Treaty Cruisers', the first of which was laid down at Fairfield, Govan on 15 September 1924. The County-class cruiser *Berwick* was closely followed by the second of the class at Portsmouth, when *Suffolk* was laid down on 30 September 1924. The Marchioness of Bristol launched her on 16 February 1926 and she was completed on 31 May 1928. Then followed the cruiser *London*, laid down seven days after the launching of the *Suffolk* and launched on 14 September 1927 by the Lady Mayoress of London. Seven days later, the wife of the Admiral Superintendent, Mrs L.A.B. Donaldson,

Portsmouth Harbour in the 1920s. HMS *Victory* is moored on the Gosport side.

laid the first keel plate of the County-class cruiser *Dorsetshire*. All of this construction work took place on No. 5 slipway.

By January 1926 the establishment of the dockyard stood at just over 13,600. This showed a slight increase due to the new building work, but in September of that year the government announced the closure of Pembroke Dockyard and the run-down of Rosyth Dockyard to a care and maintenance role. This caused much agitation in naval circles, and in particular at Portsmouth, where room had to be found in the yard for several hundred established men from the two dockyards. Some hired men in the dockyard were displaced to keep the dockyard's population within its peace-time complement and additional housing had to be found within the town for the newcomers and their families. Unfortunately this caused some resent-

ment in the dockyard and town towards the newcomers, which only time would heal. However, all through this period the dockyard was not short of work. Decommissioning the world's largest fleet was no small task, for de-ammunitioning and de-storing hundreds of vessels and finally disposing of unwanted ordnance kept the stores system of the yard fully stretched.

From September 1922 until April 1924 the battleship *Royal Oak* was under refit, her first since commissioning in 1916. Indeed, much of the battle fleet was in sore need of refit and updating. April 1926 saw the recommissioning of the battleship *Warspite* after nearly two years in which her twin funnels were trunked into one and other wartime lessons were incorporated. She relieved the battleship *Queen Elizabeth*, which had similar work carried out between May 1926 and January 1928 when she was recommissioned. During this time all the Queen Elizabeth-class battleships had their twin funnels trunked into one. The *Malaya* was in the yard from September 1927 until February 1929. *Valiant* followed from March 1929 until December 1930. At this time work was also undertaken on the battlecruisers *Renown* and *Repulse* (nicknamed 'Refit' and 'Repair'). The R-class battleships also came in for work in the yard, the *Resolution* from 1926 to 1927 and *Royal Sovereign* from 1927 to 1928. The decade ended with the battlecruiser *Hood* refitting between May 1929 and March 1931. With the added workload of cruisers, destroyers, submarines and other small craft, the yard was a hive of industry.

In the immediate years after the war, plant in the dockyard tended to be underfinanced, but by 1929 considerable progress was being made in updating plant, machinery and buildings. A start was made in rebuilding the Rangefinder Test House, Rigging House and Semaphore Tower which had been destroyed by fire in 1913. The original plan was for the Colour Loft and Sail Loft to be constructed on the north end of the Semaphore Tower but this was later abandoned. The contract for the building was awarded to Messrs Playfair Tools Ltd for completion on 2 July 1929. South Railway Jetty was reconstructed as an ongoing scheme to extend the western frontage of the dockyard.

The demand for electricity was being fuelled by the greater use of electrical furnaces in the foundries. The increasing use of pneumatic hand tools for caulking, riveting, chipping and drilling led to larger electrically driven air compressors being installed. Electric arc welding and

A picture of No. 12 Dock some time in the late 1920s, showing the destroyer leader *Wallace* (D20). Three other destroyers are docked abreast at the far end of the dock. During 1916 a need was expressed by the Commander-in-Chief Grand Fleet for larger destroyer leaders. Eight were built to an Admiralty design and five to a design supplied by Thornycroft. *Wallace* was of the Thornycroft design. She was broken up in 1946.

electrical lifting appliances, and the electrification of the main pumping station, all threw demand on a limited supply. In 1928 the Main Electrical Generating Station was modernised at a cost of nearly a quarter of a million pounds. In 1928 the station consumed 36,254 tons of coal. At this time the yard was operating fifteen dry docks and four locks that also acted as dry docks. There was also the great floating dock, known as No. 1 floating dock, built by Cammell Laird, Birkenhead in 1913. It had a lifting capacity of 32,000 tons. At the outbreak of war it was towed with No. 1 crane lighter inside it to Invergordon, where it remained until the cessation of hostilities, rendering valuable service to the Grand Fleet. The dock was safely brought back to the yard and berthed in its old position at the north end of the dockyard close to the Round Tower. The dolphins for mooring it can still be seen

today. Unfortunately No. 1 crane lighter was wrecked on the east coast. A smaller floating dock was installed at Haslar for submarine work.

In the latter part of the decade many of the workshops and plant buildings in the dockyard were receiving some form of modernisation, particularly the dockyard railway system, where tracks were relaid and extended around dockside areas to accommodate tracked cranes. In 1927, the year of the national coal strike, the yard had to turn to foreign imported coal, which was not only less efficient but proved to be more expensive than the British product. The dockyard's working population dropped in 1929 to 11,298 employees, of which 107 were women. But during this period of unease the dockyard did manage to maintain a healthy workload and build new ships, which in comparison with other parts of the country was indeed fortunate.

On 14 September 1927 the cruiser *London* had just been launched from No. 5 Slipway by the Lady Mayoress of London. Within a few days the keel plates of the cruiser *Dorsetshire* were laid. The *London* was in the second batch of the new 10,000-ton Washington Treaty cruisers. After seeing much service she was scrapped at Barrow in 1950.

Surrounded by the typical clutter of a dockyard quayside, the battleship *Queen Elizabeth* can be seen in No. 14 Dock some time between 1926 and 1928 during her first reconstruction.

Looking south towards the mouth of the harbour. The old slipways can be seen on the lower left of the picture. The event is thought to be Navy Week. In the middle of the picture can be seen the steel structure of the new Semaphore Tower, which dates the picture to 1929. The battleship and cruiser alongside are unknown. In the background can be seen the aircraft carrier *Furious*.

The newly built cruiser *Dorsetshire* leaving Portsmouth for trials during 1930. The *Dorsetshire*, in company with the cruiser *Cornwall*, was sunk by Japanese aircraft in the Indian Ocean south of Ceylon (Sri Lanka) on 5 April 1942.

On 12 January 1922 HMS *Victory* was dry-docked for the last time in No. 2 Dock after a national appeal to preserve the ship that was sponsored by the Society for Nautical Research. Work began to restore her to her appearance at the Battle of Trafalgar. The climax of the restoration work came on 17 July 1928, when she was inspected by King George V.

CHAPTER 5

REARMAMENT, 1930–9

The highlight of the year was the long-awaited opening of the new Semaphore Tower, Rangefinder Test House and Rigging House on 4 July 1930. All these facilities were encompassed within the one building, whose base spanned the roadway to South Railway Jetty and embodied the old Lion Gateway. The building replaced a similar one, built in 1778, that was mysteriously destroyed by fire on 20 December 1913. At first German saboteurs were blamed and the Admiralty offered a substantial reward for information leading to the arrest of the villains. But none were found. A rumour spread within the dockyard that seemed more probable than the skullduggery of enemy agents. Adjacent to the seat of the fire was a store containing spare furniture belonging to the Royal Yacht. We are told that it had been the habit of certain persons responsible for the furniture's safe keeping to loan out items unofficially for special occasions, and that some of that same furniture was now mysteriously unaccounted for. The rumour goes on that these individuals were apprehensive of a forthcoming inventory check and that the fire was started

deliberately on the preceding day to hide the incriminating evidence. Whatever the reason, the blaze spread uncontrollably, trapping the three men on duty in the Semaphore Tower and consuming them within its flames.

The building had been the heart and hub of the dockyard and its loss was sadly felt by the town, dockyard and seafarers using the harbour, who could no longer see weather warning cones or ship movement signals flying from the tower's mast. The First World War interrupted plans for a new building but a start was made in 1928 using the foundations of the old 1778 building. The original tower, added in 1834–5, was of wood construction, being 106ft tall. The new tower was of stone construction, with a height of 126ft. The mast for the new building was taken from the German cruiser *Nürnberg*, which had surrendered to the Grand Fleet off May Island on 21 November 1918.

The most impressive feature of the new building was the gateway. The old Lion Gate coincidently was also constructed in 1778, the same year as the original building, and formed the main entrance through the rampart fortifications to the town of Portsea, standing roughly at the junction of Alfred Road and Queen Street. When the fortifications were demolished in the 1870s the elaborate gateway was taken down and erected as the main entrance to the garrison's Anglesey Barracks in Queen Street. But when these barracks were transferred to the navy to become what was then known as Victory Barracks (now known as Nelson Barracks), the gateway was once more dismantled and offered to the town, which declined it. So the sad stones, individually marked, were placed in the Navy Works Department yard within the dockyard. There they languished until Admiral Sir Percy Grant, Admiral Superintendent of the Dockyard, suggested that as the gateway to the new Semaphore Tower would face South Railway Jetty, which was the senior jetty of the dockyard at which all royal and other dignitaries arrived and departed, the stones of the old gateway should be reassembled there as a 'Gateway of Empire'. The sentiment was quickly taken up by the city, which had long referred to itself as the 'Gateway to the Empire'.

There were three distinct ceremonies for the opening. Admiral Grant, who

had been Admiral Superintendent from 1922 to 1925, drove through the main arch to perform the formal opening. Vice Admiral L.A.B. Donaldson, the Admiral Superintendent, unlocked the door to the building with a silver key shaped like an anchor. Admiral of the Fleet Sir Roger Keyes, the Commander-in-Chief, was presented with a silver key bearing his own personal arms to unlock another doorway, after which he ascended the Semaphore Tower and declared the building open. Other dignitaries included the Lord Mayor of Ports-mouth, councillors, senior dockyard officials and service chiefs.

In 1930 the cruiser *Dorsetshire* was completed and, after commissioning, sailed to join the Atlantic Fleet. The battleship *Valiant* completed her reconstruction, and recommissioned on 2 December for service with the 2nd Battleship Squadron of the Atlantic Fleet. On 12 September 1931 a triple keel-laying ceremony took place in No. 13 Dry Dock. The destroyers *Crusader* and *Comet* were the first destroyers to be built in a Royal Dockyard; the third vessel was the Mining School

Nightingale, the mining tender to HMS *Vernon*, passing HMS *Dolphin* on her way out of the harbour on 29 April 1937. *Nightingale* was built in No. 13 Dock along with the destroyers *Comet* and *Crusader* in 1930–1. She saw almost continuous service until finally being broken up at Southampton in the late 1950s.

tender *Nightingale*, destined to spend all her life in Portsmouth, and finally sold out of service in 1958.

The 1930 discussions on the limitations of naval construction finally bore fruit when the five major maritime powers – Britain, America, France, Japan and Italy – reached agreement on tonnage and types of warship affected. The main precept of the accord was that no new battleships would be built until 1936. From the date of the agreement much of the nation's major civilian warship-building industry fell into decay, with many skilled craftsmen and designers leaving the service, a loss to be bitterly regretted when rearmament started in earnest.

For the Royal Navy it meant keeping old battleships now past their prime at the forefront of operations. The increased development of mines, torpedoes, shells and aerial bombs raised doubt as to their survivability in a modern war. In consequence of this the Royal Dockyards, and in particular Portsmouth, were to reap a dividend. On 23 December 1933 HMS *Warspite* paid off at Portsmouth to begin the first of the major battleship reconstructions. The Queen Elizabeth class was chosen in preference to the slightly newer Royal Sovereigns because of their wider beam, which added to their stability, and a slightly higher speed of 24 knots coupled with a larger radius of action. It was anticipated that the speed of battleships would increase in foreign navies when construction restarted and therefore maintaining the speed of 24 knots was considered essential.

The main problem with the reconstruction of the *Warspite* was that of adding hundreds of tons of extra armour, armaments and other equipment and still keeping the same speed with roughly the same draught and displacement. The answer was found in her machinery. Her twenty-four Babcock and Wilcox boilers were surrendered for six Admiralty-pattern, three-drum high-pressure boilers and her old engines and gearing gave way to more modern designs, giving a weight saving of 1,952 tons. With the surrender of the heavy armoured conning tower and other redundant structures, a margin of spare tonnage allowed a complete remodelling of the ship. The gutting of all machinery and boiler spaces caused much anxiety for the General Manager's Department of the dockyard, for never before had such a daring reconstruction been attempted. Removing all the weight from the middle of the vessel along with much of her bulkhead stiffening, and leaving the great weight of the ship's main armament at the fore and after ends in place, caused some deformity problems which were foreseen and proved difficult to rectify.

The ship's main armament of eight 15in guns also received a new lease of life. The elevation for each gun was increased from 20 degrees to 30 degrees, which increased the effective range from 23,400yd to 32,200yd (roughly 16 nautical miles). *Warspite* recommissioned on 29 June 1937 for the Mediterranean Fleet, but because of steering problems was not fit for service until 5 January 1938, when she finally sailed for the Mediterranean.

The failure of the Naval Disarmament Conference in London on 19 December 1934 was received with mixed emotions. For the depressed iron and shipbuilding industries of the country and many in the Royal Navy it was a glimmer of hope. For others it foretold of an impending arms race that could possibly end in another war. These fears were

The battleship *Iron Duke* in the floating dock at Portsmouth in August 1933. She was the only one of her class to survive the naval treaty of 1930, when it was agreed to demilitarise her by removing B and Y gun turrets. In this guise she acted as a sea-going gunnery training ship at Portsmouth from 1932 to 1939. In 1939 she served as base ship at Scapa Flow and as flagship of the admiral commanding Orkney and Shetland. She was sold to Metal Industries in 1946 for breaking-up.

increased when in March 1935 the government published 'A Statement Relating to Defence', a White Paper recognising the need for rearmament. The aggressive rise of the Nazi Party in Germany hung like a shadow over Europe. Small wonder then, that the signing of the Anglo-German Naval Treaty in June of that year, which allowed Germany to build up to 35 per cent of the size of the Royal Navy, was hailed as a triumph for sound reasoning. Sadly the triumph was chilled by the expansionist activities of the Italians in Ethiopia, an area of British interest. Within ten days of the Anglo-German naval agreement, a peace ballot by the League of Nations showed that 90 per cent of the people favoured multilateral disarmament. It must have seemed to many that the runaway train could not be stopped. In those dark days the dreams of men were giving way to a reality which was to have far-reaching consequences, for a prototype of the Hawker Hurricane fighter began its trials and Robert Watson-Watt successfully carried out the first experiments with radar.

On 16 July 1935 the eyes of the world focused on Portsmouth as the Royal Navy gathered its strength to celebrate the Silver Jubilee of King George V. In that historic anchorage of Spithead the navy assembled 157 warships. With over sixty merchant ships of various sizes and hundreds of small craft, it was an impressive show of strength. The assembly of such a large number of ships naturally presented its own problems, many of which landed on the doorstep of the dockyard. On occasions such as this the Admiral Superintendent of the Dockyard acted as host to large numbers of VIPs from the Admiralty and government, foreign representatives and in particular the royal family. It was to be expected that the dockyard would be extremely busy over this whole period, but for many areas of the country still in the grip of depression the review seemed an extravagance. Sadly the old king had but six months of his life left. A new king would, for a short time, take his place.

In December 1936 Portsmouth and its dockyard were again in the world's press. On 10 December King Edward VIII abdicated in favour of his brother, the Duke of York, who acceded to the throne as King George VI. The following day the ex-king was created Duke of Windsor. Two hours after speaking to the nation and the world of his 'final and irrevocable decision', he travelled through the darkness of the night to Portsmouth, entering the dockyard by the Unicorn Gate, and there without state or ceremony boarded the destroyer *Fury*. Escorted by the destroyer *Wolfhound*, the once King and Freeman of the City of Portsmouth, a man much loved by the nation and admired throughout the world, sailed at 2.00 a.m. for Boulogne and the loneliness of exile. Ironically, one of the last landmarks of old England he would see was the column of the Naval War Memorial at Southsea, which he had unveiled on 15 October 1924.

The mid-1930s proved to be a busy period for the dockyard. With the normal refits and dry-dockings of the fleet throwing heavier demands on the labour force, labour had to be found for the reconstruction of *Warspite*. On 2 September 1936 the battlecruiser *Renown* entered the dockyard to start her reconstruction, which was to last until August 1939. The battleship *Queen Elizabeth* commenced her reconstruction on 1 August 1937, which proved to be

On 12 January 1934 the battleship *Nelson* ran aground on Hamilton Bank in the approach channel to Portsmouth Harbour when leaving for exercises. It was an embarrassing incident for the Royal Navy and in full view of Southsea beach. When dockyard tugs failed to pull her off, a number of destroyers were commanded to steam past in the hope that their wash would assist the tugs in refloating her. She remained aground until the next high tide, by which time the press had all the photographs they wanted.

more extensive than that of the *Warspite*. Despite all these demands the dockyard continued a programme of new construction, with the cruiser *Neptune* being laid down in September 1931 and launched on 31 January 1933. The destroyer leader *Exmouth* was launched on 7 February 1934, followed by the launching of the cruiser *Amphion* on 27 July. The cruiser *Aurora* was launched on 20 August 1936, and on 6 April 1938 the keel plate of the cruiser *Sirius* was laid down. The pace of naval rearmament was steadily increasing, although with strict controls imposed by the Treasury, which was adamant that rearmament would not jeopardise the country's recovery.

In July 1935 the Government outlined in a circular to local authorities plans and duties falling upon them in the advent of air raids in a possible future war. The plan called for, among other things, rescue squads, bigger fire services, first-aid centres and anti-gas stations. It was suggested that public bombproof shelters were considered impractical and that house owners should provide their own blast protection. Although it was not until January 1937 that Portsmouth appointed a special committee to report on such matters, as the year progressed the dockyard and public in general became familiar with the letters 'ARP' (air-raid precautions).

On 16 July 1937 Portsmouth and Southampton civic authorities organised an exercise in which the dockyard was bombed and casualties sustained in the dockyard and city. From midnight until 3.00 a.m. while most of the population slept, a blackout was imposed with all street lighting extinguished and traffic proceeding with dimmed lighting. Five hundred volunteers, in addition to paid emergency services and other local permanent staff, carried out various tests and exercises, which included dealing with cut water, gas and sewage mains, house fires and forty-eight casualties. The whole exercise was watched by Sir Samuel Hoare, the Home Secretary, Mr Geoffrey Lloyd, Parliamentary Secretary to the Home Office and Sir Philip Game, Commissioner for the Metropolitan Police. Over twenty officials from the Home Office acted as umpires and many other cities, towns and government departments sent delegates to witness the operation. After the events of the night, Sir Samuel Hoare congratulated Portsmouth and Southampton for being two of the pioneering municipalities in this work. With the close cooperation of the navy and the army garrison, Portsmouth set about organising its civilian army, which would eventually number many thousands of its citizens and was to see the city better prepared for the ordeal to come than most of the country.

During the month of May 1937 the eyes of the world once more fell upon Portsmouth and its dockyard as it began to fill with all types of warships requiring varying degrees of attention gathering for the Coronation Fleet Review of King George VI. One hundred and sixty ships were majestically assembled at the Spithead anchorage on 22 May as the King, accompanied by the Queen, steamed through the lines of warships in the Royal Yacht *Victoria and Albert*. That special place held in most British hearts for the Royal Navy was amply demonstrated when 190,870 people flooded into the dockyard for 'Navy Week'.

By 1937 it was clearly seen that, as the proposed naval building programme gathered momentum and new ships began to join the fleet, many of the dockyard's departments would be stretched to capacity. The boat-building and repair facility was centred around the old Mast Pond (1665) at the southern end of the yard and comprised four buildings. The newest building was No. 6 Boathouse, built in 1845–8. No. 5 Boathouse was then a masthouse and so was part of No. 7 Boathouse. The oldest was No. 4 Boathouse, said to date from 1690 to 1700. It was a wooden building similar to the present-day Nos 5 and 7 Boathouses and stretched from the canal to the old Prison Cells. It was obvious that these facilities could not cope with the demands of an increasing fleet. The city at that time proposed a new traffic layout for that area, in which Queen Street was to be widened. A large traffic island was planned for the site of the Victory Gate, necessitating its demolition as well as that of the old Porter's Lodge (1708 – the oldest building in the dockyard), the Prison Cells (1882) and the Ship & Castle

The Silver Jubilee Review of the Fleet by King George V on 16 July 1935. One hundred and fifty-seven warships and sixty merchant ships formed the spectacle, together with hundreds of other craft. At 10.00 p.m. the Fleet was illuminated and the firework display began. The picture is taken from Southsea Common, overlooking the Naval War Memorial.

public house. A new gateway into the yard was to be built and a new No. 4 Boathouse would stretch from the canal to the new gateway. The Second World War curtailed most of this planned development.

However, a start was made in the latter part of 1937 on demolishing part of the old wooden No. 4 Boathouse. Unfortunately the demands of new ships coming into the fleet were already being felt. It was decided to demolish the northern part of the building and on the site build the first half of the new building, leaving the southern part of the old building in commission to alleviate some of the shortfall in boat repair facilities of the yard, and also to

house the craftsmen who worked in the building. In 1939, £150,000 was the total estimate for the work, with a further £14,000 allocated for machinery. However, before the building was half-finished the country was at war with Germany. The southern exposed and unfinished end of the new building was quickly given a temporary corrugated-iron-sheeting end wall and hastily pressed into service, with the expectation of finishing the construction work at the end of hostilities or when the crisis permitted. The building is still today (2005) in its unfinished state.

The deteriorating political climate in Europe led to the mobilisation of the

The battleship *Nelson* lying at South Railway Jetty after her grounding and being de-stored in preparation for inspection in dry dock. Sailors and marines are unloading 16in shells from one of the ship's magazines.

Royal Navy on 27 September 1938, but by 30 September the nation was breathing a sigh of relief as the Prime Minister Neville Chamberlain returned from meeting Hitler, Mussolini and Daladier of France at the Munich Conference, greeting Chamberlain with cries of 'Peace' and 'Appeasement'. Such was the feeling in the dockyard and city that on 3 October 20,000 people assembled in the Guildhall Square for a 'Thank God for Peace' service, with the massed bands of the Royal Marines, attended by the Lord Mayor, aldermen and councillors. The lesson for the service was read by the Commander-in-Chief of Portsmouth, Admiral of the Fleet the Earl of Cork and Orrery.

With the increasing length of planned battleships and aircraft carriers, ways were sought to expand the refit berths around No. 3 Basin. In 1939 a start was made on lengthening the south-eastern side of the basin. A cofferdam was erected and a pocket was created between No. 12 Dry Dock and the eastern wall. The longer battleships never materialised and the pocket

became affectionately known as 'mucky corner'. As the last summer days of August 1939 slipped away, so did the last hopes of peace. When on 1 September Britain demanded that Hitler stop his invasion of Poland few, if any, realistically thought that the great war machine set in motion could be stopped. As 11.00 a.m. ticked by on 3 September and the Prime Minister announced to the country that it was once more at war with Germany, many felt total despair, but still clung to the faint hope that reason would prevail. But for many others there was a feeling of 'Well, now let's get on with it'. None could imagine the terrible sacrifice in men and ships that the Royal Navy would be called on to make, and none could foresee the heartache, despair and destruction that would descend on the dockyard and the city of Portsmouth.

HMS *Warspite* in July 1937, in her new guise after rebuilding at Portsmouth Dockyard during 1934–7. She left Portsmouth on 5 January 1938 to become flagship of the Mediterranean Fleet. The red, white and blue identification stripes can be seen on B turret. These were applied to RN ships operating from Gibraltar at the time of the Spanish Civil War.

The dockyard was a large community made up of people of many crafts and skills, working in offices, storehouses and workshops, many of whom formed their own clubs or societies such as fishing, cycling, football, bowling, shooting, darts, drama, etc. During the festive periods their children were treated to days out and parties. The picture shows the Drivers' Café on The Hard on 7 January 1939 at the Christmas party of 'Welburns' (welders and burners). It was to be the last occasion of such treats before the Nazi storm descended.

Opposite, above: The battleship *Queen Elizabeth* at Spithead in July 1935. She was the senior flagship of the 1935 Silver Jubilee Review. She would be back in the dockyard on 1 August 1937 to commence a reconstruction that would completely alter her appearance.

Opposite: In 1938, to improve the dockyard's boat-building and repair facilities the old wooden boathouse opposite the Mast Pond was demolished to make way for the building of the existing No. 4 Boathouse. The new building was planned in two stages, the north end to be built first followed by the southern end. This enabled work still to be undertaken in the southern part of the partially demolished wooden boathouse. The picture shows the remains of the old building in the background with the work under way on the floor of the new building in the foreground. In the bottom left of the picture can be seen the lock gates to the tunnel that connects the Mast Pond to the harbour.

At 6.30 on a bright sunny morning in July 1939, Mr Wright of Wright & Logan, naval photographers, stood on Point Beach, Old Portsmouth to capture HMS *Renown* putting to sea for trials after her complete rebuilding in the dockyard. The dockyard trials party can be seen at the back of B barbette and the base of the fore funnel. It was the custom not to repaint ships until after they had completed their trials. *Renown* was sold to Metal Industries Ltd in August 1948 for breaking-up.

CHAPTER 6

THE SECOND WORLD WAR PERIOD, 1940–50

The Munich crisis of 1938 had set in motion much of the machinery needed for the commencement of war and by the beginning of 1940 Portsmouth was a hive of industry. But for the dockyard and port it was to be a war like no other. Many of the tasks that befell the dockyard were the same as in previous continental wars: the safe passage of the army to France, assisting with the organisation and work to resist invasion, maintenance of anti-invasion flotillas, assisting with raiding and patrolling the enemy coastline, setting up and maintaining the boom defence of the anchorages along with associated flotillas of inner and outer patrol craft, wreck and damaged-ship recovery, and the conversion of vessels for trials and experimentation. It was also found necessary to convert many of the older warships as well as hundreds of merchant ships, to new wartime roles.

The need for additional shore training establishments for naval personnel also put a heavy burden on the dockyard staff. The Portsmouth Command was to stretch from Newhaven to Portland and as far north as Haslemere. As the size of the Royal Navy grew so did the workload of the dockyard. The dock-

yard's boundaries were firmly trapped by the city of Portsmouth and, as in the First World War, it found its capacity limited and in consequence took over other industrial sites in the Portsmouth Command. Outstations stretched from Bournemouth to Brighton and the dockyard drafted many of its workforce to these locations as overseers, instructors or key players at the new sites. Even today, with pay and muster books open to study, it is still difficult to assess the total dockyard wartime population, but it is generally thought to have exceeded 40,000.

The effects of German bombing brought a new threat to the dockyard, which for centuries had been regarded as a safe haven. The repair or demolition of bombed buildings and plant in the dockyard often demanded a large labour input. The construction of bombproof shelters, fortified slit trenches, first-aid centres, control and rescue units and ARP posts added to this. Later on, there were requirements to provide the dockyard Home Guard battalions with magazines, patrol posts and machine-gun pillboxes on nearly all the jetties, and a need to enlarge and disperse the dockyard fire-fighting service into smaller units scattered around the yard. This saw a constant stream of civil construction work going on around the dockyard. The early months of the war saw a steady flow of work from accidental grounding, collisions, mechanical breakdowns and, later, damage through enemy action, which was eventually to swamp the repair facilities of the yard.

The secrets of the German magnetic mine had been mastered by Lieutenant-Commander Ouvry and his team from HMS *Vernon*. Experimental counter-measures had been secretly carried out on the Canoe Lake at Southsea, which in turn eventually led to the fitting of degaussing coils around ships' hulls to neutralise their magnetic field so as to avoid detonating magnetic mines. Trawlers were hastily converted in the dockyard for mine-sweeping, which became a major task in the channels and approaches as German bombers could sow magnetic and other types of influence mines at night, rendering the harbour and anchorage unusable to shipping. In consequence any large splash or water disturbance was instantly reported and investigated and the Minewatch organisation became a valued part of the harbour security.

The shortage of cruisers to guard against commerce raiders led to a number of large, fast merchant ships undergoing conversion in the dockyard to armed merchant cruisers. Some of these were to return later in the war for conversion to other roles for the invasion of Europe.

The evacuation of the army from the Dunkirk beaches between 27 May and 4 June 1940 affected every port along the coast and Portsmouth was to play its part. Everything that could steam was added to the growing flotilla of ships plying between the beaches and Dover. The Hayling Island ferries, Isle of Wight steamers, Pickfords small coasters, Dutch trawlers that were in the dockyard, tugs and even small boats from warships in refit were added to the armada. Block-ships were prepared and, with a small squadron, sailed on 8 June for Dieppe, where they were successfully laid. The same date saw an order to the Commander-in-Chief of Portsmouth to organise the evacuation of troops from the Le Havre district, and the dockyard and surrounding harbours and creeks were scavenged for boats. Captain Coppinger, DSC, RN, the Captain of the Dockyard, took the dockyard tugs across, all with cutters in tow. Anything that would float was hastily repaired and an odd assortment of about 200 craft made up the armada.

With all Europe now in enemy hands, the fate of the free world depended on whether Britain would stand. The prospect of invasion now became a reality. On 24 May 1940 a three-page secret message was sent to the Commander-in-Chief Naval Home Command, giving instructions for im-mobilising dockyards and the destruction or removal of plant and machinery, stores, fuels, weapons, ammunition and communication networks. Arrangements were made for armed resistance by service personnel ashore and afloat, and cooperation with the army. These were indeed very dark days.

As the majority of the European coastline was now accessible to the Germans, it was not long before enemy air attacks started on convoys, patrol craft and minesweepers using the coastal shipping lanes. Dockyard tugs were often called to rescue disabled or burning vessels and tow them into the dockyard. The first air raid on the dockyard came on 11 July. The bombers were very high and little damage was done to the yard but the city suffered about eighty casualties. During this period the dockyard and anchorage was filled with fishing boats, merchant ships and warships from Holland, Belgium, Norway and France, most of them with their crews. Ships that were in the process of fitting out in these countries were also towed to

The AA cruiser HMS *Sirius* seen here entering Portsmouth some time after the war. *Sirius* had been built in Portsmouth, having been launched by Lady James, the wife of the Commander-in-Chief Portsmouth, on 18 September 1940, and completed for sea on 6 May 1942. She was scrapped at Blyth in 1956.

Portsmouth to prevent them falling into enemy hands. For the Commander-in-Chief their crews presented a problem as many wanted to go home. For the dockyard, it meant additional work. Many of these ships were old and worn out and spare parts were almost non-existent. Also their armaments were different calibres from those of British warships and they had to be rearmed. It would take time to sort out the political problem that these ships and crews

presented and find a role for them within the Royal Navy.

Today it is difficult for modern generations to understand those terrible years of the Nazi bombing campaign. Much has been romanticised in books and films, which has clouded the terror and sheer fatigue suffered by the people at that time. There were sixty-seven bombing raids and 1,581 alerts. The alerts were almost as destructive to the dockyard as the raids, for they stopped work often for many hours at a time. Night-time alerts robbed workers of sleep, many of whom would have been at work all day and spent most or part of the evening on fire watch, ARP or Home Guard duties. At the height of the blitz on Portsmouth, absenteeism and late mustering in the dockyard were extremely high. Much was through sheer fatigue, but often roads around the dockyard were blocked by rubble and it was impossible for public

A snowy winter scene at Royal Clarence Yard. The picture is thought to have been taken in 1944 and shows some of the many small craft involved in the victualling department. Note the harbour launch in the lower left-hand corner bearing the sign 'Boom Defence'. This would refer to the anti-submarine boom that ran from the Lumps Fort area in Southsea over to the Isle of Wight. Its concrete block can still be seen today at low tides.

Looking north-east from the 240-ton crane in No. 3 Basin on 25 May 1944. The bow of the armed merchant cruiser *Ranpura*, which was in the dockyard being converted into a heavy repair ship, is on the left of the picture. The submarines are *Tireless* and *Token*, built in No. 13 Dock and here being completed, and the hulk of the French submarine *Ondine*. The collier is the *Yewdale* (1929), which had arrived the day before from Blyth. The dock is Admiralty Floating Dock No. 11. The Round Tower has a Bofors anti-aircraft gun mounted on top.

transport to maintain routes or time schedules.

During this grim period 6,626 properties were totally destroyed. Another 75,435 properties were seriously or slightly damaged, and many buildings were damaged more than once. More than 40,000 bombs or mines of various types descended on the city and dockyard, although thankfully many hundreds more fell into the harbour and surrounding sea. In the city, 930 people were killed and 2,837 injured, many of them seriously. Sadly, there appears to be no record of numbers killed and wounded in the dockyard, although many casualties were suffered by both civilian and service personnel. The main object of these attacks, the dockyard, was sorely hit on many occasions and every major building suffered bomb damage. During the great raid of 10 January 1941 the heart of the city was virtually destroyed. The Commander-in-Chief, Admiral Sir W.M. James, ordered 1,000 sailors from the command to assist in clearing the streets and set up his 'Friendly Aid Parties'. These were small parties consisting of a leading seaman or corporal and four men, distributed around the streets that had been blitzed to assist dazed citizens in recovering their treasured possessions from the bombed buildings. These men with their strong arms and cheerful smiles did much to maintain morale in the city.

It was on occasions such as this that the city received great help from the dockyard and the naval command. For although the dockyard was badly damaged, its facilities were freely given to the city in many small ways, even to temporarily supplying electrical power from its generating station when the city's own was bombed.

In the midst of an attack on 24 August 1940 the destroyer *Acheron* had her stern blown off. Repairs were quickly effected and by 17 December she was at sea south of the Isle of Wight running speed trials, when she struck a mine in a previously swept area. She sank with heavy loss of life.

Another tragedy befell one of the fifty American 'Lease-Lend' destroyers, HMS *Cameron*. On the night of 5 December 1940 she was in No. 8 Dry Dock when she was blown over on her side during a particularly nasty raid. The dock had to be flooded to avoid fire and possible explosion. She became a constructive total loss and was stripped of her armament and useful fittings. The hull was used for structural experiments and eventually discarded at the end of the war. The battleship *Queen Elizabeth* had been rebuilding at Portsmouth since August 1937 and was in the process of final fitting-out and trials. Because of bombing, this was out of the question. She left Portsmouth in the early part of

December 1940 and completed her final trials at Rosyth in January 1941. The battleship *Nelson* was in C Lock of the dockyard from 15 January until 25 April for repairs to mine damage and sailed without mishap on 6 June 1940. *Ark Royal* was in D Lock from 19 February until 1 March for recoating her bottom. The battleships *Resolution* and *Revenge* and the County-class cruiser *Berwick* were all receiving attention of one sort or another during March 1941. The *Berwick* was moored on the promontory under the 240-ton hammerhead crane when during the early light of morning and after a heavy raid, a large parachute land mine fouled the crane when descending and could be seen dangling close to the cruiser.

Throughout this bombing period there was a reluctance to send large, important warships to Portsmouth, where they ran the risk of being damaged or destroyed in dry dock. On 2 May 1941 a Naval Stores Department memo headed 'Dispersal of Stores' stated that additional storage had been found at Brighton and other inland areas for high-value and important stores. The demand for radar and other such inventions was now being met and the risk of having them destroyed while waiting in storehouses to be fitted was too great.

The light cruiser *Sirius* was laid down on No. 5 Slipway on 6 April 1938 and was launched on 18 September 1940 by Lady James, wife of the Commander-in-Chief. This caused great anxiety for the dockyard management as an air raid during the launch would have been disastrous. However, she did suffer bomb damage from near misses during fitting-out. She was completed on 6 May 1942. Sirius, reputedly the brightest star in the heavens, is also the star on the Portsmouth City crest. During March

1942 Portsmouth held a Warship Week to raise money to 'buy a warship'. Over £1,200,000 was raised and consequently *Sirius* became Portsmouth's adopted ship, being presented with plaques and other gifts from the city before she sailed.

On 1 July 1942 Admiralty Floating Dock No. 18 was launched from the main slipway, and was followed almost a year later by AFD 21. Both docks were 2,750 tons displacement and designed for escort vessels up to the size of a destroyer. They saw service in many parts of the world. On 1 July 1943 Miss Clarke, the sister of Vice-Admiral Marshal Llewellyn Clarke, CB, DSC, Admiral Superintendent of the Dockyard, laid the keel of the cruiser *Hawke* on No. 5 Slipway. This ship was cancelled in March 1946 and the hull broken up on the slipway. The submarine *Tireless* was laid down in No. 13 Dry Dock on 30 October 1941 and was followed on 6 November by the submarine *Token* in the same dock. Both were floated up on 19 March 1943 and completed in 1944. These were followed by the submarines *Thor*, on 5 April 1943, and *Tiara* on 9 April, both of which were flooded up on 18 April 1944. They were never completed as fitting-out was stopped in 1945, and they were discarded in 1946 and 1947 respectively.

During the later part of 1942 the dockyard became involved in the work of mast-making for the destroyer programme. In April of 1941 five flotillas of destroyers (forty ships) were ordered by the Admiralty; known as the 7th to 11th Emergency Flotillas, they later became the U, V, W, Z and CA classes of destroyers. The first to enter service was HMS *Grenville*, the flotilla leader of the U class, followed by HMS *Ulster*. They were completed with the traditional tripod mast but new radar sets entering service were proving difficult to mount. Consequently in November 1942 the Director of Signals Division announced that the tripod mast would be replaced by a tall lattice mast in the new destroyer programme. The first batch of twenty masts to the new design were prefabricated in Portsmouth Dockyard and sent to shipyards engaged in destroyer construction around the country.

During all this period hundreds of minor war vessels received new equipment, were refitted or had battle damage repaired. It is at this point interesting to look at the dockyard's dry-docking register for those years:

1939........243 vessels
1940........271 vessels
1941........195 vessels
1942 ....251 vessels
1943........242 vessels
1944........877 vessels
1945........286 vessels

With the air war over Britain slowly being won by the Royal Air Force, the pace in the dockyard quickened as the invasion of Europe loomed closer. The dockyard became the home of many innovative ideas for the Normandy landings, not all of them as successful as the designers hoped. The idea for a floating blow-up roadway was tried out in the locks and the harbour, and a lot of time and labour were devoted to this project. Inflatable lifting bags for the repair of landing craft on the beach were tried in No. 4 Boathouse in the same bay (No. 4) where one of the first prototype midget submarines had been built in October 1942. Much experimental work on the basic landing craft design was done in the dockyard, where experiments could be conducted in secret.

Looking north across No. 3 Basin, 25 May 1944. The AMC *Ranpura* is alongside the inner wall with the incomplete hulls of the submarines *Thor* and *Tiara*, which were built in No. 13 Dock. They were cancelled before completion and broken up. On the outside of the wall (Fountain Lake Jetty) are a number of British Yard Minesweepers (MYMS) and motor minesweepers (MMS). In the trots are LCTs (tank landing craft armed with a number of light anti-aircraft guns for use as flak ships). A large number of infantry landing craft (LCI (L)) can be seen and on the extreme right the old Royal Yacht *Victoria and Albert* acting as an overflow accommodation ship. The Naval Gunnery School at Whale Island can be seen in the background.

Consequently many strange shapes emerged as specialist craft.

After the Dieppe raid of August 1942 it was realised that the invasion forces would have to take a port with them. The testing tanks at Haslar and the dockyard Mould Loft and Drawing Offices often found they were preparing odd-looking shapes for testing, even though thoughts of a second front were a dream for the future. The code name for this port was 'Mulberry'. It was in fact two ports: Mulberry A for the American beach and Mulberry B for the British beach. The dockyard, along with other shipyards all over the country, embarked on a construction programme the like of which the world had never seen. One hundred and forty-seven concrete caissons, known as 'Phoenix', were used in the two ports, although more were built to cope with losses. The Phoenix caissons ranged between 1,600 to 6,000 tons, and their construction consumed 1½ million tons of concrete and up to 70,000 tons of steel. Twenty were

Looking north-west across No. 3 Basin, 25 May 1944. The cruiser *Achilles* (of Battle of the River Plate fame) is in D Lock completing a refit. The four LCTs along the inner wall are nos 853, 685, 665 and 784. In the Pocket is the former monitor *Marshal Soult*, launched in 1915 and later hulked as a harbour base ship. Lying on the inside by the large crane is HMS *Sultan*, launched in 1870 as an armoured central-battery ship and reduced to a harbour service hulk. On the extreme left of the picture can be seen the stern of the cruiser *Scylla*, which served as flagship of Rear Admiral Philip Vian, commanding the Eastern Naval Task Force at the Normandy landings. In the middle distance can be seen the *Foudroyant* (1817) and the *Lupin*, launched in 1916 as an escort sloop but reduced to an accommodation ship for riggers.

built in the dockyard, using the locks as building berths. The foreshore of Horsea Island in the harbour also had slipways built for the construction of Phoenix. Units of the Whales, the code name for the floating steel roadways and pierheads, along with Bombards, the floating steel breakwaters, were also constructed in the yard and in addition the dockyard also prepared some of the Gooseberries. This was the code name for old, redundant ships that would sail to Normandy under their own steam and then be scuttled to form breakwaters to protect the Mulberry harbours.

Petrol, the lifeblood of a modern army, would be in constant demand once the armoured formations broke out of the invasion box. To satisfy this need it was proposed to lay pipelines from Sandown bay to Querqueville, to the west of Cherbourg. This operation was given the code name 'Pluto' (Pipe Line Under The Ocean) and again the dockyard was called on to undertake much of the experimental and final construction work. Some of the pipework involved continuous welding, which up until that time had never been done. A great deal of experimenting had to be carried out on different types of steels and welding techniques before success was achieved. There were two types of pipeline. Harmel was the name given to the flexible steel pipe laid on to floating drums 50ft in diameter, from which they unreeled as the drums were towed along. Hais was a flexible pipeline laid by cableship. In all, ten pipelines were laid, delivering over 210 million gallons of fuel to the thirsty Allied forces.

The Dieppe raid had shown the need for a bombardment weapon to swamp the enemy defences and destroy the morale of the defending troops. From this sprang the Landing Craft Support (Rocket), originally known as the 'Grasshopper Craft'. These were LCT Mk 3 converted to fire 1,080 rockets. The experimental work and first conversions were carried out in No. 2 Basin of the dockyard and the first trial firing conducted at Spithead on 11 April 1943. During these trials hard lessons were learnt, like dispersing the colossal heat generated by batch-firing of rockets in the well of the landing craft, which at times was in danger of cooking the crew. Finally the problems were solved and the rocket craft became a fearsome weapon in the D-Day arsenal.

In the run-up to the Normandy invasion, the sheer scale of the preparations started to tell on city and dockyard alike. The dockyard railway system began to groan under the weight of thousands of tons of materials coming into the yard. The mooring department of the yard and the Port of Southampton had to find an additional 3,000 berths in the command for landing craft, and moorings for 2,300 other vessels. The city and surrounding area, already bursting with stores and men, was required to provide an additional 29,000 billets for personnel.

During the assembly period, the victualling department at Clarence Yard was called on to supply quantities of provisions for the waiting armada. The flow of harbour craft supplying the invasion fleet with these stores greatly increased and queuing-berths had to be provided for vessels loading stores. Traffic became so congested in the harbour and channel approaches that on 5 June 1944 a memo was issued, giving notice of the introduction of traffic control signals in the form of flags by day and lights by night, to be hoisted at Semaphore Tower, HMS *Vernon*, HMS *Hornet*, Fort Blockhouse, sub-signal stations at the north end of the dockyard and Horse Sand Fort. These signals controlled the flow of traffic in one direction, either all in or all out.

The naval armaments departments at Frater and Bedenham on the Gosport side of the harbour had grown to over 800 acres by 1943 and were employing nearly 4,500 people. Some 20,000 tons of ammunition had been set aside for the bombarding force alone. The fleet of ammunition lighters, barges and tugs supplying the armada swelled the already congested waters of Spithead. As one old tug man complained, 'It's not the trip out and back that's the problem, it's finding the right boat once you're out there.'

With the commencement of the invasion, a constant stream of damaged craft flowed into the dockyard and during the months that followed a staggering 550 craft were dry-docked in the yard. When LST 63 was dry-docked in A Lock, the Docking Register gave the reason for docking as 'Holes in bottom caused by sitting on Sherman tank', an unusual, if amusing, variation on the reason usually given: 'Damage Repairs'. With the procession of damaged ships also came a continuous flow of casualties from the ships and beaches, although much lighter than had been expected. Far larger were the solemn columns of German prisoners.

The end of 1944 saw a reduction in the naval commitment to the war in Europe. It had been decided at the Allied summit meeting of November 1943 in Cairo that the British would send a fleet to the Pacific. Accordingly the dockyard, in company with other yards, found itself preparing large numbers of warships of all classes for war in the Pacific, as warships were steadily sent east to join the East Indies Fleet and the British Pacific Fleet for the final drive in the war against Japan.

No mention of the end of hostilities seems to exist in the General Orders for the Dockyard or Naval Stores memos, except for orders relating to the cancelling of overseas shipments. However, on 15 May 1945 an order was issued for Fire Guards in the dockyard to return their steel helmets and sleeping bags to No. 19 Store. Those wishing to retain their sleeping bags or who had lost them were to be charged four shillings.

The city, however, did rejoice on VE night. A white ensign which had been flown from the Guildhall on Armistice Day in 1918 was rehoisted on a pole from the ruins of the Guildhall, and sailors climbed the burnt-out tower to ring out the Pompey chimes. But these celebrations were nothing in comparison to VJ Day. On 15 August, just after the Prime Minister had finished his broadcast announcing the end of the war with Japan, the city went wild. The shrieking hooters and ships' sirens in the port became incessant, the smallest dockyard craft joining in with the largest of the navy, although a port order limiting the celebratory noise to one hour could be said to have been roughly complied with. Bells were rung, fireworks and rockets exploded in the air and searchlights from military establishments and ships danced in the night sky. Bonfires were lit on street corners and bombsites and there was singing, laughter and dancing in the streets. The people immersed themselves in the good-humoured jollifications that only come at great moments like this. Thousands packed the Guildhall Square and along with the celebrations in the city streets the revelry went on into the small hours of the morning, when many of the people went to bed thinking, 'It's over at last.'

For more than five years the burning drive of the dockyard in keeping with the rest of British industry was 'to win the war' and this great machine could not be stopped overnight. The fleet still had much to do in making the world safe, bringing home our war prisoners, occupying enemy-held territory, clearing millions of mines from the sea lanes and helping to rebuild countries so that our servicemen could come home. Winning the peace would be almost as demanding as winning the war. The same problem that arose after the First World War now reared its head again: that of stopping a machine and converting it to produce peacetime goods for home consumption and export.

Peace did not mean that the amount of work for the dockyard slackened. Hundreds of ships were returning home and their crews were looking forward to demobilisation. Many of the unwanted landing craft were driven on to the beach at Tipner, north of the dockyard. Eventually this line of grounded ships stretched from Tipner to Portchester Castle. Soon every creek and spare water channel that could take a boat at high tide was in use to moor hundreds of motor launches, motor torpedo and gun boats, corvettes, frigates, submarines and destroyers. The larger ships such as cruisers, depot ships, aircraft carriers and battleships, were moored in the harbour or at Spithead. It would take time to remould the Royal Navy, with nearly 5,000 hulls afloat, to a peacetime force.

Immediately after the war the service financial vote was drastically cut. This meant that many of the dockyard's bombed buildings would have to be left in their ruined state, while most of the outstations directly connected to the war effort were closed and the drafted personnel returned to the dockyard.

However, the war was instrumental in removing a great nuisance from the dockyard: the 'Marlborough salient'. This was a 5-acre area of land north of Bonfire Corner which protruded into the dockyard as far as No. 8 Dry Dock; it was here that the original Marlborough Gate stood. The old police station can still be seen there today. There were plans as early as 1938 to take this area into the dockyard boundary, but the destruction of houses on the site by German bombing hastened that decision. By 1944 the authorities had moved Marlborough Gate to the new position at Bonfire Corner, which had originally been the apex of a bastion in the fortifications surrounding the dockyard, erected under the direction of Sir Bernard de Gomme between 1665 and 1668. De Gomme served King Charles II as Chief Engineer of all the King's Castles in England and Wales.

In 1945 the dockyard also took over the land to the east of Unicorn Road just outside Unicorn Gate. These little streets, each with a public house on the corner, were well known to the sailors and dockyard men. The effects of the Nazi bombing campaign did much to render this land waste. At first only small enclosed areas were used to store mooring anchors, buoys and cable, but eventually the Unicorn Gate would be moved and all this area enclosed within the dockyard.

Over the next four years the dockyard would hardly change. It was to be a time of contracting and regrouping, of sorting and resettling. Pictures of the period show dark, sooty buildings still bearing the scars of war. It was to be an uneasy peace, still with the wartime shortages in food, clothing and building materials. Food rationing lingered on in the postwar years until it finally ended in 1954.

Looking south across No. 3 Basin, 25 May 1944. On the left is No. 13 Dock, containing two LCT Mk 4 tank landing craft. In No. 14 Dock are two LCT Mk 3s, while No. 15 Dock accommodates two LCT Mk 4s. Alongside the wall is the destroyer *Porcupine* in two halves. She was torpedoed by U-602 on 9 December 1942 and brought back to Portsmouth, where she was unofficially known as 'Pork' and 'Pine'. She later acted as a base ship for landing craft. She was never repaired. Outside the *Porcupine* is the Mk 5 tank landing craft LCT 2042. In the distance can be seen the city's power station and the Isle of Wight.

Looking west across No. 3 Basin, 25 May 1944. The large ship in C Lock is the old battleship *Centurion* being prepared as one of the D-Day blockships that were known as 'Corncob'. She was scuttled on 9 June 1944 as part of Gooseberry 1, a component of the Mulberry Harbour. The destroyer *Jervis* is in B Lock. Rear Admiral Vian's flagship, HMS *Scylla*, can be seen in the top left of the picture. She was called 'the toothless tiger' because of her comparatively light anti-aircraft armament. On 23 June *Scylla* ran over a German acoustic mine off the Normandy beaches and sustained massive damage to her midship section. She was brought back to Portsmouth, where she remained in her damaged state until discarded in 1950. On the left of the picture can be seen the Lease–Lend Captain-class frigates *Trollope* and *Lawford*, with the repair ship *Artifex* behind.

Looking west across the northern corner of No. 2 Basin on 26 May 1944. No. 2 Ship Fitting Shop is on the far side of the basin. Almost hidden behind the landing craft is the submarine P 556. Formerly belonging to the US Navy and transferred to Britain under the Lease–Lend agreement, she is seen here in care and maintenance. P 556 was handed back to the USN in the latter part of 1944 and sold to shipbreakers H. Pounds; on 24 January 1949 she was beached in Portchester Lake, where she remained for many years. The steel racks and pickling ground for No. 3 Ship Building Shop and the slipway can be seen in the upper right of the picture. Pickling was the process whereby steel plates and angle iron were immersed in large tanks of diluted acid to remove mill scale prior to painting.

Opposite, above: Another view from the top of the 240-ton crane taken on the same day. The destroyer *Jervis* is in B Lock, while A Lock and No. 9 Dock are empty. On the inner wall of the basin is the Mk 2 tank landing ship LST 322. Alongside her is LCG(L) 1062, an LCT Mk 4 fitted with two ex-destroyer guns for engaging shore batteries.

Opposite: Looking south-west across No. 2 Basin on 26 May 1944. The destroyer *Escapade* is along the wall undergoing lengthy damage repairs, with the frigate *Stayner* alongside her. On the south wall are two Mk 4 tank landing craft and to the right can be seen the bow of the tank landing ship LST 320. The *Victory* can be seen in the middle background. During the war period her mast and yards were struck down. The dry dock in the foreground is No. 11 Dock. The caisson has been removed and can be seen in the left-hand corner.

The south-eastern corner of No. 3 Basin looking towards Unicorn Gate. Most of the buildings outside the gate have been reduced to shells by German air raids. In the background can be seen the burnt-out remains of the Guildhall. Note the camouflage netting over the tank deck on some of the landing craft.

Looking towards the Pocket of No. 3 Basin in which can be seen the old monitor *Marshal Soult*. The 240-ton floating crane was originally German, being part of the First World War reparation.

The south-west wall of the dockyard on 26 May 1944. The steam tug in the foreground is discharging ash into the lighter. Beyond is the Lease–Lend Captain-class frigate *Lawford*, fitted out as headquarters ship for Assault Group Juno 1. She was bombed and sunk by German aircraft off Normandy on 8 June. Outboard of her is the *Trollope* and the tank landing ship LST 302 with the paddle tug *Grappler* alongside. In the background is the repair ship *Artifex*.

An aerial view of Portsea and the dockyard taken in 1947 from the nose of a Fleet Air Arm aircraft. Portsea lies shattered by German bombing; most of the buildings are still standing but reduced to shells. Many of the dockyard buildings also show signs of the bombing. But in those austere years there was still hope for the future.

CHAPTER 7

THE COLD WAR PERIOD, 1950–60

In 1945 massive cuts were made in defence expenditure and hundreds of ships were sold or scrapped. The years of uneasy peace that followed the Second World War saw the rise of nationalism in many of the countries of the old Empire, much of it sown with the seeds of communism. The position in Europe was not dissimilar to that of 1939, with the main threat coming from the Soviet Union.

War, if it came, would demand of the Royal Navy much the same as in 1939–45: mainly the protection of the Atlantic convoys. In consequence the Royal Navy retained large numbers of escort vessels in all the home ports. In 1947 Portsmouth had seventy vessels laid up. The headquarters for this fleet were on the old depot ship HMS *Resource*, moored at Fountain Lake Jetty. The maintenance of these ships was a time-consuming task for the 180 officers and 2,400 other rates, as well as the dockyard workforce. At that time Harwich had 99 ships, Plymouth 80, Forth 60, the Clyde 15, Sheerness 23, Chatham 20 and Pembroke 50 – in all some 417 vessels, although some had been earmarked for sale.

It was thought at the time that technology would not advance greatly in the course of the next few years because of underfunding. This affected not only Britain but all the maritime nations of the world, and if existing ships were pressed into service much of their equipment would still be of operational use. Work in the dockyard during this retrenchment period was mainly dry-dockings and annual refits.

In June 1948 the Soviet Union showed its intentions by cutting all road and rail links to Berlin through East Germany, forcing America, Britain and France to establish the Berlin Airlift. In April the following year the North Atlantic Treaty Organisation (NATO) was formed. The banding together of European nations with America and Canada for mutual protection against a would-be aggressor showed once more a threat to peace, just four years after yet another war that was meant to end all wars.

On the evening of 14 July 1950 Portsmouth Harbour and the surrounding populated areas were rocked by a violent explosion. Six lighters loaded with ammunition at the Bedenham pier of the Royal Naval Armaments Depot had exploded. Fifty minutes later a further violent explosion shook the area. The pier, surrounding vessels and buildings were damaged, along with hundreds of windows in the Portsmouth, Gosport and Fareham areas. Needless to say, the huge pall of black smoke rising in the sky above the harbour and the widespread broken glass, with the occasional door off its hinges, brought alarm, cries of sabotage and even fears of the possibility of war to everyone in the harbour area.

Strategically, it was thought that the Soviet Union would not contemplate an aggressive action in Europe until she had developed her own atomic bomb and built up a stockpile. With this in mind, it was accepted that 1952–3 was the earliest that the Soviets could develop such a weapon, so the year of a potential war would probably be around 1957–8.

The Soviet Union exploded its first atomic bomb in 1949, thus upsetting the West's timetable, and in 1950 Communist North Korea invaded South Korea, heralding the Korean War. The West saw these as the possible opening gambits of World War Three. On 27 June 1950 the Prime Minister, Clement Attlee, pledged support for the UN in resisting the invasion of South Korea and by September of that year the first British troops were in action near Pusan, with a sizeable Royal Navy presence in the surrounding waters. In November China intervened on the side of North Korea. As the war escalated, so the military position of the West in Korea became more critical. On 4 December Attlee flew to Washington to urge the Americans not to use atomic weapons. To prevent a military reverse, the West increased its military commitment to the Korea campaign and Britain, in company with other Western powers, embarked on a rearmament programme which none could afford.

On 10 October 1950 the fleet aircraft carrier HMS *Victorious* was taken in hand at the dockyard. She entered D Lock on 12 December 1950 for the largest reconstruction of a warship ever undertaken in a British yard. It was not until 12 December 1955 that she finally took to the water again. The flooding-up

HMS/m *Affray* was one of the A-class submarines, which were mainly designed for service in the Far East but arrived too late for war service. *Affray* was commissioned in 1946. She was based at HMS *Dolphin* when she was lost with all hands in the English Channel on 17 April 1951.

was carried out with great care and attention to detail for it was estimated that a list of more than one and a half degrees would cause the sponson of the new angled flight deck to strike the coping of the lock. But a completely upright undocking was achieved after four and a half years on the blocks. She finally commissioned on 14 January 1958, costing £20 million.

Concern had been steadily mounting over the underwater speed of submarines, and it was realised that escort vessels built during the war would not have sufficient speed to catch modern submarines. To bridge this gap the Royal Navy converted many of the war-built fleet destroyers to fast AS frigates. The first of these fully converted destroyers, known as Type 15 anti-submarine frigates, were the *Relentless*, converted at Portsmouth Dockyard and the *Rocket*, converted at Devonport. The destroyer *Verulam* followed *Relentless*. The destroyer *Troubridge* was to be the third destroyer conversion but work was stopped at the fitting-out stage and the ship was towed to J. Samuel Whites at Cowes where she was finished.

On 17 April 1951 the nation heard that His Majesty's Submarine *Affray* was overdue. As time drifted on, hope was eventually given up for her crew. This was a sad occasion as she was based at HMS *Dolphin* and was a familiar sight in Portsmouth and Gosport, where many of her crew lived. The Docking Register for the yard shows she entered B Lock on 12 March 1951 for an Intermediate Docking, and undocked on '4-5-51'. It is unusual for a mistake to occur in the Register as it is checked by more than one person, but this is borne out by the next entry for docking in B Lock which was bar vessel *Barndale* on '5-4-51'. It would seem that the 4 and 5 in the date were reversed; *Barndale* must have entered the lock on the same day that *Affray* came out.

It was announced on 14 June that *Affray* had been found on the edge of the Hurd Deep in about 200ft of water. It was HMS *Vernon*'s diving trials ship HMS *Reclaim* that found *Affray* and the first use of an underwater television camera gave the nation the eerie pictures of her conning tower. The disaster was attributed to a fracture in the snort mast, although mystery still surrounds the exact cause. Within eighteen months No. 1 Ship Shop in the dockyard was prefabricating a number of stronger snort masts.

On 6 February 1952, with the death of King George VI, the country once more had a queen. Queen Elizabeth II's coronation was held on 2 June 1953. However, prior to the coronation, the Queen Mother visited Portsmouth on 29 April 1953 to unveil the 1939–45 extension to the Naval War Memorial at Southsea, on which 15,000 names of those of Portsmouth Command who had no known grave except the sea were inscribed. Over 18,000 people packed the Common to pay tribute to their loved ones.

On 15 June 1953 the spotlight once more fell on Portsmouth as the Queen reviewed her fleet at Spithead, where, in HMS *Surprise*, which was acting as a royal yacht, she steamed past 14 miles of warships. The naval might of Britain was on show to the world. During the Coronation Review of her father King George VI in 1937, 125 aircraft travelling at 85 knots overflew the fleet. At the 1953 review over 300 aircraft of the Fleet Air Arm cruising at 350 knots flew in formation past their Queen. During the afternoon news was flashed to the fleet that Her Majesty's

The new frigate *Leopard* on the morning of 23 May 1955, the day of her launch by Princess Marie Louise. She was the first ship to be built in Portsmouth after the war and with the launching came the hope for better things to come. *Leopard* was classed as a Type 41 AA frigate. She was completed for service on 30 September 1958 and eventually scrapped in 1978.

Submarine *Andrew* had made naval history by crossing the Atlantic from Bermuda, a distance of 2,840 miles, entirely underwater. For a conventional submarine this was an incredible achievement. At 10.30 in the evening the Queen pressed a golden key and simultaneously over 200 ships blazed into brilliant illuminations. The grand finale of the day was the firework display, started by a single rocket fired by the Queen from HMS *Vanguard*. The climax, however, was a final salvo of 2,500 rockets that lit up the night sky and surrounding beaches, on which it was estimated that over a million people had gathered from all parts of the globe.

The workload that fell on the dockyard because of this great assembly of ships can well be imagined. The Queen ended her message to the fleet with the following words: 'I know how greatly the dockyards and their supporting services have contributed to make this Coronation Review an occasion which I shall long remember. We send our best wishes to you all and I look forward to further visits which I hope to make to you in the future.' As the fleet dispersed, many departed for ports around the kingdom on flag-showing visits as part of the coronation celebrations.

One of the high points for the dockyard came in 1953 with the keel-laying of the first warship to be built there after the war. HMS *Leopard* was a Type 41 anti-aircraft frigate. She was the first prefabricated, all-welded warship to be built in the yard. The bow was built in No. 1 Ship Shop and only scraped through the doorway with inches to spare when leaving the shop for the slipway. The ceremony was performed by Mrs A.G.V. Hubback, wife of the Admiral Super-intendent, who switched on an automatic welding machine to join two weldments of the lower part of the ship together. *Leopard* was launched on 23 May 1953 by Her Royal Highness the Princess Marie Louise. The ceremony went without a hitch in perfect weather and the new warship entered the waters of the harbour amid the cheers of nearly 10,000 people. To prevent bad luck the Princess borrowed a coin to pay for the scissors which she used to cut the tape in the naming ceremony. *Leopard* commissioned on 30 October 1958. The first sections of the Type 12 AS frigate HMS *Rhyl* were laid on 29 January 1958 and she was launched fifteen months later.

For Britain this was a difficult decade and the Royal Navy was constantly reacting to various flashpoints of potential danger around the world. On 13 June 1956 the last British troops left the Suez Canal Zone. President Nasser's nationalisation of the canal on 26 July brought much anger and fear to many countries in the Western world. The fact that Russia was supplying large quantities of arms to the Egyptians did not help and many feared that Egypt, with its precious canal, would become a satellite of the Communist Bloc. Britain and France embarked on a plan to reoccupy the Canal Zone. Reservists were called back to the colours and selected ships were taken out of 'mothballs' (the name given to the Reserve Fleet).

The dockyard and its support services found this an intensely busy period. But during the slow build-up to the landings that occurred on 5 November, world opinion turned against Britain and France. The UN, and America in particular, condemned the Anglo-French action and the pound plummeted against the dollar as fighting along the Canal Zone halted under intense international pressure. By the first week of December

On 10 October 1950 the fleet aircraft carrier HMS *Victorious* was taken in hand at the dockyard. She entered D Lock on 12 December 1950 for the largest reconstruction of a warship ever undertaken in a British yard. The photograph shows one of her new boilers being lowered into place.

British and French troops started to leave Suez. Petrol rationing was introduced in Britain and the country's relationships with the rest of the world, particularly America, were soured and seemed as though they would never recover. In the dockyard, ships returned home and many were returned to the 'Mothball Fleet'. The invasion was the first time a helicopter assault had been mounted from an aircraft carrier and was to shape the Royal Navy's amphibious thinking for the future. The aftermath of the Suez Crisis also saw a most radical defence review, which was to have far-reaching consequences and take the armed services into the Nuclear Age.

Throughout the decade the government slowly increased spending on the navy and also on plant for the dockyard. Many of the old machines that did valiant service throughout the two world wars were now slowly being replaced, but the yard still bore the signs of bomb damage from the 1939–45 conflict. It would take another decade before most of the affected areas were rebuilt. But the well-earned dockyard reputation of 'can do' still prevailed and between 1950 and 1960 nearly 2,050 vessels of all types were dry-docked or slipped, a figure that clearly shows the large volume of work that flowed through the yard at that time.

Fort Blockhouse at the entrance to Portsmouth Harbour was the home of HMS *Dolphin*, the Royal Navy's submarine base at Gosport. The picture is believed to have been taken some time in the late 1950s.

HMS *Victorious* in D Lock in 1956. The armoured flight deck and island have been completed. The large overhang of her angled flight deck necessitated dismantling the old dockside crane and building a new one with a longer jib to plumb the centre of the lock when working. The track for the new crane can be seen being laid at the right of the picture.

Opposite, above: The date of this picture is unknown but thought to be in the late 1950s. It shows women workers of the dockyard employed in the Colour Loft making flags. From the decorations it would appear to be near Christmas time.

Opposite: This photograph was taken to show piling work on the jetty between the Pocket and D Lock. In the background can be seen the *Leviathan.* She was one of six Majestic-class light fleet aircraft carriers built at Vickers Armstrongs (Walker) and launched on 7 June 1945. Work was suspended on her after the war and she was towed to Portsmouth, where she was moored in the Pocket for many years. *Leviathan* remained in this unfinished state until she was disposed of in 1968, by which time much of her equipment and machinery had been cannibalised for the benefit of other carriers.

In this 1960 view HMS *Victorious* shows
a fine turn of speed after rebuild.

All aboard for the launch. The last members of the launching party board the frigate *Rhyl* on the morning of her launch on 23 April 1959. *Rhyl* was one of the Royal Navy's successful Type 12 AS frigates. She commissioned on 30 October 1960 and was said to be a very happy ship. She was expended as a target in September 1985.

Opposite, above: Members of the Works Department assembling timber shoring in preparation for strengthening Fountain Lake Jetty. On the No. 3 Basin side of the jetty can be seen the AS frigate *Urchin*, with a Battle-class destroyer outside her.

Opposite: Looking down the slipway at the first keel section of the general purpose frigate *Nubian*, which was laid on 7 September 1959. The battleship *Vanguard* is lying alongside the jetty at the end of the slip.

CHAPTER 8

THE ATOMIC AGE,
1960–70

During these years there were changes in the dockyard, but they were subtle and slow. The large coaling depot at the end of the yard, close to the floating dock, had lost its coal although the dwarf walls of the concrete bays were to remain for many years to come. Coal as a means of producing power had been replaced, mainly by electricity. In 1928 the annual consumption of coal for the generating station alone was just over 36,000 tons and the consumption for fires, cranes, forges and steam-powered craft, etc. was about 18,000 tons. However, over the last twenty years there had been a steady decline in the use of coal. Its storing and distribution was a labour-intensive and demanding issue when compared with electricity, and the early-morning lighting of fires and the removal of tons of clinker and ash were a messy and irksome business.

The main craft in the dockyard was that of the shipwright. It was through that department that the stairway to higher dockyard management began. But since the introduction of iron ship-building into the Royal Dockyards, the blacksmith had begun to rival the shipwright in numbers and workshop facilities. The war had seen an expansion in the use of electric arc welding, which had robbed the smitheries and foundries of much of their work, for it was less labour-intensive to prefabricate complicated fittings from flat steel plate, rather than forge or cast them. During the war, unskilled people, including many women, became competent welders with only a few weeks' training. The skills of the riveter and his squad were also in decline; many of the old riveted, wartime-built ships were being paid off and replaced by all-welded ships, as it slowly became the norm of naval construction. However, welding was still viewed with misgiving by many in the shipbuilding industry; the memory of welded wartime-built ships suddenly fracturing along a welded plate, causing them to break in half, still lingered on in their memories. Out of these fears was born the Non-destructive Test Centre, the department responsible for X-raying and other means of testing welded connections.

It was during this period that the Ministry of Defence (Navy) was created. The system of three service chiefs each operating from their own service ministry was gradually phased out in

The Victory Gate, formerly known as the Main Gate, was built between 1704 and 1711, along with the dockyard brick wall, and replaced the ramparts, moat and palisades raised by Dutch prisoners of war under Sir Bernard de Gomme in 1666–7. The gateway lost its elaborate iron scrollwork and lantern when it was widened by 12ft in 1943 to allow wider loads access into the southern end of the yard. The brickwork to the entrance of the old Police Cells was removed and the pier to the gateway was jacked up and slid on a roller pathway to its new position. A new wicket-gate was then built, connecting it to the Police Cells.

favour of a more centralised administration. This was brought about partly through the need for economy and partly by lessons learnt during and just after the war, when it was found that many of the operations invariably involved more than one service and that joint planning was essential. For the Royal Navy and the Royal Dockyards, both steeped in the tradition of the old Admiralty (often pronounced 'Admer-ralat-tee' by old dockyard men), it was a move viewed with many misgivings.

Civil engineering work in the Royal Dockyards was performed by the Navy Works Department of the Admiralty, in some ways an unsung department which over the years produced many fine buildings and prided itself on its finished product. As one of the departments of the yard, it had a close working relationship with the ship departments. On 1 April 1963, after 168 years of service to the Admiralty, the department was transferred to the Ministry of Public Buildings and Works.

HMS *Rhyl* commissioned for service on 31 October 1960. She was the only one of the successful Type 12 AS frigates built in the dockyard. But shortly before, on 6 September, the dockyard launched the *Nubian*, a Type 81 (Tribal-class) general purpose frigate. She completed on 9 October 1962, exactly thirteen months after the first section of the Leander-class frigate *Sirius* was laid down on the slipway. She was launched just over a year later on 22 September, but before she completed for service in June 1966, the first sections of keel plating of HMS *Andromeda* were laid on 25 May that year. There were twenty-six ships in the class, reputedly the finest postwar frigates built. The last ten ships had their beams increased by 2ft and were known as the 'Broad-beam Leanders'; *Andromeda* was one of these. She was launched in brilliant sunshine, a year after the first keel sections were laid, on 24 May 1967 and completed on 2 December 1968.

Andromeda was one of the quickest-built of her class and was completed ahead of time. The dockyard had high hopes of more frigates being built on that historic slipway, which had seen the birth of the battleship; ships such as the *Inflexible*, *Devastation*, *Formidable*, *Britannia*, *Dreadnought*, *Neptune*, *King George V*, *Iron Duke*, *Queen Elizabeth* and *Royal Sovereign*, to name but a few. None of the cheering assembly that gathered around the slip-

At 10.30 a.m. on 4 August 1960 Britain's last battleship HMS *Vanguard* was released from her moorings in the harbour to commence her last voyage to the breakers' yard. It was a solemn occasion with no flags, cheers or ships' sirens. Only the boys on the training ship *Foudroyant* raised a cheer as she came past. As she approached the harbour mouth the tugs could not hold her 45,000-ton mass and she gently slid to one side, grounding outside the Still & West public house at Old Portsmouth (dropping off the ghosts of old mariners and mateys, it was said). After frantic efforts by the dockyard tugs she was freed to continue her final journey. And so ended a chapter in history that had made Portsmouth the envy and wonderment of the world in the building of great battleships.

way on the day of her baptism could ever have imagined that she would be the last warship to be built in the dockyard, and that the historic slipway would eventually be filled in and made into a car park. Not even a plaque would mark the birthplace of these famous ships that had at times turned the course of history.

Refits and conversions are the backbone of dockyard work and from 1959 to 1960 the aircraft carrier *Bulwark* was converted to a commando carrier, to be followed in 1961 by a more extensive commando carrier conversion of her sister ship *Albion*. In 1963 the *Bulwark* underwent further work to bring her up to the standard of the *Albion*. The aircraft carrier *Centaur* was in refit during 1963 and again in 1965. Refits were also carried out on *Hermes* and *Victorious*. The destroyer *Agincourt* was converted to a fleet radar picket during 1960 and the depot ship *Maidstone* was extensively converted into a nuclear-powered-submarine sup-port ship between 1958 and 1962. During this period the A- and T-class submarines could be seen occupying Nos 7 and 10 Dry Docks undergoing refits. Also the first refits of the Porpoise-class submarines were com-pleted. The late 1950s and 1960s also saw a large amount of work on the Ton-class minesweepers in conversions of engines and adapting them to the role of minehunters. No. 9 Dry Dock became known as the 'rock and roll dock'. Instruments had been placed in the bottom of the dock for measuring and calibrating the magnetic signature of Ton-class minesweepers. First, the funnel was removed and then a wooden platform erected across the minesweeper. On instruction the crew ran from side to side to produce a rolling motion on the

vessel. Later, the rolling of the vessel was achieved by a hydraulic arm mounted on the dockside and bolted to the hull.

One of the major jobs of the dockyard during this time was the conversion of the cruiser *Blake* to a command helicopter cruiser between 1965 and 1969. The light fleet carrier *Triumph* became a familiar sight in the dockyard when she was converted to a heavy repair ship over a seven-year period. Work was suspended on her for long periods while commitments to higher-priority work were met. She finally commissioned for service on 7 January 1965.

The Government announcement in 1966 cancelling the two projected aircraft carriers and their four escorts brought a sense of gloom for the future to many in the dockyard. It had already been planned to build a new dry dock in the yard to accommodate the super-carriers. A ghost of this project lived on in the shape of HMS *Bristol*, one of the four planned escort destroyers, which had been too far advanced in her building to cancel.

To mark the twentieth anniversary of the NATO alliance, a review of sixty-one ships from twelve NATO countries was held at Spithead on 15 June 1969. The Queen with the Duke of Edinburgh and Princess Anne embarked in the Royal Yacht *Britannia* at South Railway Jetty, after which the vessel steamed slowly out of the harbour past the thousands of people lining the beaches. Twenty-one-gun salutes were fired from HMS *Vernon* and HMS *Dolphin*. Then, as *Britannia* approached the lines of assembled ships, the thunder of further salutes roared out from eighteen of the ships in the review lines. Many thousands more people gathered on the shore surrounding the historic Spithead anchorage, where at night the NATO fleet presented a pleasing

An aerial view of No. 1 Basin in 1960. The Basin and Nos 5 and 6 Docks were originally built in 1698 and are the oldest stone basin and docks in the world. The other docks were built at the turn of the nineteenth century when the basin was enlarged. It has been said that together they represent one of the greatest legacies left by the sailing-navy era. The docks are numbered from left to right, with HMS *Victory* being in No. 2 Dock. The warship on the jetty is HMS *Devonshire*.

spectacle with its illuminations. After the review twenty-one of the ships entered the dockyard and were open to visitors. Over the two-day stay, 50,000 people visited the ships.

On 9 September 1969 another step was taken in breaking down the barriers into the male strongholds of the dockyard when five female apprentices were indentured as electrical fitters. It was a move heralded with many mixed feelings among the craftsmen of the yard; but as in the war, it was found that women in the right place and taught the right skills were just as competent as the men.

All through the 1960s the naval vote had steadily increased but the number of ships in the active fleet had gradually fallen. This did not seem to be reflected in the workload of the dockyard, for between 1960 and the end of 1969 it had dry-docked or slipped 1,990 vessels of all types. Sixty-seven vessels less than the previous decade. Since the end of the war the labour force of the dockyard had been in a steady decline. At the start of the decade there were nearly 14,000 in the General Manager's Department alone, but by 1969 the figure stood at 11,100. There are a number of reasons for the reduction. There was a willingness on the part of the MOD to allow the numbers to fall in keeping with the predicted future workload of a much smaller Royal Navy. Portsmouth in general had, since the end of the war, become an attractive industrial area where a highly skilled labour force could be lured with bigger incentives than could be achieved in the dockyard. The Royal Navy had now become a highly technical force. It was to be expected, and indeed at times encouraged, that smaller industrial sites devoted to defence equipment should spring up in the Portsmouth area.

The dockyard had experienced a good year in 1969, with the majority of its

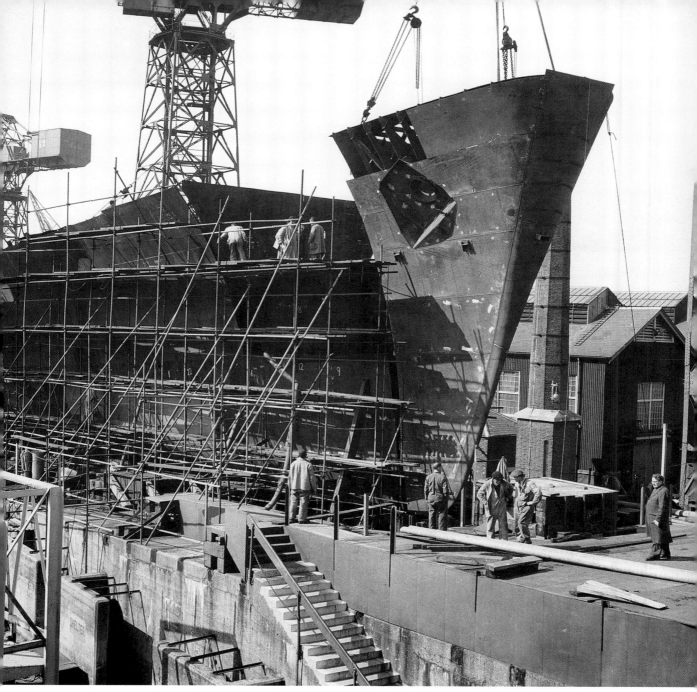

The prefabricated bow section of the new Tribal-class frigate *Nubian* being gently lowered into position on No. 5 Slipway on 11 April 1960. *Nubian* was launched on 6 September 1960 and commissioned on 9 October 1962. Sadly she was expended as a target in 1987.

planned work completed on time and in some cases ahead of schedule. Many 'firsts' were chalked up: the first Broad-beam Leander to be handed over to the navy, the first long refit of a Type 12 frigate com-

pleted, on HMS *Yarmouth*, and the first long refit of a Type 81 frigate completed, on HMS *Ashanti*. The first fourteen-week refit on a Leander (HMS *Sirius*) was completed on time and within cost, and

Work is well under way on the new Fountain Lake Jetty on 12 April 1962. The old Victorian jetty can be seen to the left of the picture. The grab-hopper dredger *Servitor* is lying alongside the unfinished jetty. She was built in 1935 by Fleming and Ferguson Ltd of Paisley at a cost of £37,000 and for many years was part of the dockyard scenery. She made her last trip on 29 May 1976. The Bay-class frigate to the right is HMS *St Brides Bay*, which was completed on 15 June 1945. She was sold to Shipbreaking Industries and scrapped at Faslane on 3 September 1962.

was the *Sirius*'s first refit since her building. At that time the future of the dockyard looked bright. But for some the closing of the decade was marked with sadness, for on 8 February 1969 Brunel's Block Mills closed their doors for the last time. The Block Mills were built in 1803 to the design of Brigadier General Sir Samuel Bentham, KSG, Inspector General of Navy Works, although much of the detailed planning of the building is thought to have been done by Simon Goodrich, Bentham's deputy. The machinery was in the main designed by Marc Isambard Brunel with some machines being the product of Bentham. These were made by Henry Maudslay of London. Strangely one of the original machines bears the casting marks and letters of the Portsmouth Dockyard Foundry.

The Block Mills have the proud title of the world's first mass-production factory, producing over 100,000 pulley-blocks a year. During the Crimean War in 1854 production peaked at 140,000 blocks. On closure of the building some of the machinery was installed on the first floor of No. 6 Boathouse, where a small block-making workshop was set up. Sadly some of these famous machines were destroyed, but others found their way into various museums. It was well noted by the yard men that most of the machinery was as good as the day it was first installed, 166 years previously.

HMS *Triumph* leaving Portsmouth on 1 February 1965 at the start of her first Far East tour as an escort maintenance ship. Her conversion lasted over seven years, but for a period of five years work was stopped as other demands on the dockyard were met. Although she was converted to a heavy repair ship, much of the heavy repair machinery was placed in a state of preservation and her main role became that of an escort maintenance ship, which included maintenance of helicopters.

The old Ropehouse (1776) was rebuilt in 1960. Prior to 1960 it was 1,095ft 9in in length, for many years one of the longest buildings in Europe. It was completely gutted and the old double-apex roof replaced by a steel-trussed, single-span roof. The end walls were rebuilt and large, folding, steel doors were installed to meet modern transport requirements.

Opposite, above: Admiralty Floating Dock 60 being built in C Lock in April 1965. It had a lifting capacity of 6,000 tons and was mainly intended for use by nuclear submarines. The cradle and centre-line blocks are in the process of being fitted.

Opposite: An aerial view of the south-western part of the dockyard taken in the late 1960s. In the bottom of the picture can be seen the cranes of No. 5 Slipway. The building with the square centre chimney is the old Smithery (1852). At the top of the chimney can be seen the two buildings making up the famous Block Mills (1803), which finally closed on 8 February 1969. Slightly to the left in No. 5 Dock is a coastal minesweeper undergoing conversion to a minehunter.

111

On 22 September 1964, a beautiful sunny day, the frigate *Sirius* slid down the historic No. 5 Slipway and into the waters of Portsmouth Harbour amid the cheers of dockyard men and spectators. *Sirius* completed for service on 15 June 1966 and became, like her predecessors of that name, the adopted ship of Portsmouth.

An aerial view of the western side of the dockyard taken in the late 1960s. In the top left corner of the yard can be seen the old No. 3 Ship Shop and the slipway. To the right an aircraft carrier thought to be HMS *Centaur* is in D Lock. The ship Basins 1, 2 and part of No. 3 can easily be seen.

CHAPTER 9
CUTS! CUTS! CUTS!
1970–80

The start of this decade was full of foreboding for the future. The government had decided to abandon the navy's East of Suez role by evacuating the bases at Bahrain and Singapore, and to do away with fixed-wing aircraft carriers by 1971, thus reducing the navy's capability almost solely to NATO commitments. In 1968, when these announcements were made, it was hoped there was time for a rethink or that a crisis would emerge that would defeat the plan. To the Royal Navy as a balanced force it was a major blow. The people of the dockyards knew from past experience that any political decision affecting the strength of the Royal Navy was bound to have a knock-on effect in the Royal Dockyards.

The opening year of the decade saw the twenty-fifth pantomime performed by the Combined Drawing Office Sports and Social Club in the Victory Theatre of the Naval Barracks from 21 January to 24 January. Their new version of *The Pied Piper* was another startling success for the amateur dramatic group, whose first production was in 1939. The war years brought a temporary halt to the shows, known in the city as 'the Dockyard Pantomime'; but with hostilities at an end, the old 'show must go on'

thespian tradition re-emerged and over the years the event had steadily gone from strength to strength.

On many occasions the dockyard has been described as a town within a town, and as in any town, rubbish collection and disposal are the least-mentioned subjects. In February 1970 a paper appeared, giving details of a staggering 13,000 tons of rubbish collected each year in the yard, an amount equal to the weight of four Leander-class frigates. Collecting vehicles clocked up 41,000 miles in the dockyard on their rounds. On many occasions they complained that their collecting routes were blocked by parked cars. Gone were the days of what the city called 'the charge of the Dockyard Light Horse', which referred to the in- and out-mustering times of dockyard men, when thousands of cyclists surged through the dockyard gates, blocking the roads. The cycle was giving way to the car; in 1970 there were 2,600 registered car parking spaces in the yard, but each day over 9,000 privately owned cars came on to the site. It was to be a problem of consistent concern for the authorities. Sadly the social atmosphere of cycling to work with hundreds of other cyclists would be lost.

Looking south over No. 3 Basin from Fountain Lake. The
nearest destroyer in the left-hand corner is HMS *Cavalier*.
An unknown Type 15 (full conversion) frigate is in the
middle and on the wall is a County-class guided missile
destroyer. D86 is HMS *Agincourt*, and HMS *Barrosa* is
outboard. The stern of the Tribal-class frigate
HMS *Mohawk* is in the right-hand corner. The picture is
thought to date from 1968–70.

On 15 September 1971 Flag Officers of the Royal Navy holding the position of Admiral Superintendents at Royal Dockyards were restyled as Port Admirals. In Portsmouth Rear Admiral P.G. LaNiece became known as Flag Officer Spithead and Port Admiral Portsmouth.

In March 1972 the General Manager of the dockyard, Mr H.J. Fulthorpe, declared a major redundancy, under which 137 men would lose their jobs over the next twelve months at Portsmouth. The General Manager referred to the 1969 Defence White Paper, which called for the Royal Dockyards to reduce their labour force by 5,000 by the mid-1970s. It was the first time since the 1930s that a state of redundancy had been declared in the yard. This was the start of an uneasy period which erupted at the pay talks in late June and July of that year, when a £1.50-a-week rise offered to government workers was rejected, leading to industrial action. Portsmouth, in common with other dockyards and establishments, banned overtime and night-shift working and established a strict work-to-rule. This also led to a number of one-day walk-outs and mass meetings inside and outside the dockyard. It was not until the end of September that the Naval Base unions agreed to call off their restrictive practices while the disputed national pay claim went to arbitration. Not all the dockyards and establishments suspended their ban, however, and pickets from other establishments appeared at the dockyard gate in an effort to persuade their yard colleagues to take a more determined line. In an interview the General Manager explained that 'it is not going to be easy getting back to normal and it will probably be another three to four weeks before we know exactly the state of play on every ship'.

Many of the older men in the yard, who had not known such a period before, expressed the feeling that 'never had they experienced such mistrust and bad feeling between dockyard men and government bodies'. Unfortunately these unpleasant occurrences over pay disputes were not to be the last and would reappear in 1978 and 1979.

The 1970s was a period when many of the old and, in some ways, friendly buildings would disappear as an air of change swept through the yard. On 3 March 1973 the large and antiquated Boiler Shop locked its doors for the last time. The increasing use of the gas turbine engine in naval propulsion, leading to repair by replacement, meant less work for the skills of the boilermaker, and the land on which the building stood was allocated for a new Combined Workshop. April saw the closure of the Saw Mills and the old Saw Sharpening Sheds.

On 11 February 1976 the new Combined Workshop was opened by the Chief of Fleet Support, Vice Admiral Sir Peter White. This event marked the end of a major operation for the Yard Services Manager's Department, which had been given the task of moving 150 machines into the building, some weighing as much as 50 tons. The boilermakers were the first to move in, followed by the shipwrights, along with smiths, welders, iron caulkers, drillers, locksmiths, painters and other associated skills. In his opening speech the Chief of Fleet Support gave assurances for the future of the dockyard, saying that nearly £100m was being spent on the Naval Base and dockyard to bring it up to date to meet the very full programme of naval work for the foreseeable future.

The previous home of the shipwrights, No. 3 Ship Shop, had been built in 1844 as 80ft-high covering sheds for the slipways on which wooden ships were constructed. With the beginning of iron ship production in the yard, the covered slipways were filled in and the sheds converted to plating and erection shops to serve No. 5 Slipway, where the iron vessels were built. The smiths taking up residence with their colleagues in the new Combined Workshop had been housed in Nos 1 and 2 Smitheries, the former built in 1852 and the latter around 1890.

In 1977 another old friend of the yard disappeared when it was officially announced on 5 December that the rail link connecting the yard to Portsmouth & Southsea station would close, ending 130 years of faithful service. At its height during the 1950s, 8,500 wagons a year would enter the dockyard carrying thousands of tons of materials and stores. By 1970 it was said that the yearly traffic of wagons into the yard was averaging only 700. The decline was foreseeable with the reducing demand for coal, the absence of thousands of tons of steel with the loss of ship-building, and the greater reliance on motor transport. The last train out of the dockyard left on 30 November 1977. Ironically one of the longest loads to leave the yard for some time had left just two days earlier, carrying four 100ft-long pontoons, which were made in the yard for Portland Naval Base. The presence of the railway still lingers on in the yard in the shape of its railway lines, over 25 miles of which were laid in the yard, and thought by many to be a curse on the cycling dockyard man.

Haslar Gunboat Yard, situated south of Haslar Creek on the Gosport side of the harbour, was part of the dockyard and officially came under Ship Group 1 Division. Built in 1856–8 to service gunboats and smaller craft just after the Crimean War, its layout was years ahead

Looking north along the Parade. Long Row, also known as the Terrace (1717), is on the right behind the trees. The first building on the left is the old Mould Loft (1891), next to the Joiners' Workshop (1912). At the far end of the road can be seen the old Brass Foundry (1845). With the exception of the Brass Foundry most of these buildings were demolished to make way for Victory Building, the Second Sea Lord's offices.

of its time and ranks as one of the dockyard's most inspired legacies of Victorian thinking in small-craft maintenance and management. On 26 May 1978 the yard closed just a few days after unslipping the last boat to use the facility, MFV 119. Because of its location it was often regarded by many in the dockyard as an outstation for the lost legion. This was quite untrue and extremely unfair to the ninety or so men who worked there, of which probably 50 per cent resided in Gosport. On average seventy-five boats a year were slipped or refitted in the yard to a high standard of workmanship and pride, which is often the case with small, compact yards such as this. Sadly no record can be found of the enormous amount of work performed by the yard during the war years, when hundreds of motor torpedo boats, motor gunboats and other minor war craft were slipped and repaired from HMS *Hornet*, the Coastal Forces base, which recommissioned as an independent command on 1 October 1940 and was finally vacated on 31 October 1958.

In July 1978 the new Royal Maritime Auxiliary Service (RMAS) Maintenance and Support Centre was opened by the Director of Marine Services, Captain J. Taylor, RN (retd). The complex was designed by Arup Associates of London and was highly commended for its design, incorporating the old Round Tower, which formed part of Frederick's Battery. It was originally built in 1844–8, on the north-eastern side of No. 2 Basin and moved to its present location during the 1870s' extension of the northern part of the yard. Part of the land was later used as the old coaling depot of the yard, which had now ceased to be used. This complex took over some of the work from Haslar Gunboat Yard.

During September 1979 the cranes on the slipway were demolished to make way for the North Corner development, in which most of the buildings in the area were demolished and Nos 1, 2 and 5 Slipways filled in. The North, Middle and South Slip Jetties would be rebuilt into a new, continuous jetty with modern services. Stores, facilities for crews, offices and workshops would be built to serve as the North Corner Group for service personnel of the Naval Base.

One of the achievements had been the conversion of the destroyer *Matapan* to an underwater trials ship, which started in January 1970 and finished with her commissioning on 2 February 1973. The conversion of the Leander-class frigate *Arethusa* to carry the Ikara missile system was another success for the yard. The dockyard had performed well in its refits of large guided missile destroyers and frigates. The new Type 42 destroyers had started to emerge from their building yards and brought hope for the future when it was announced that Portsmouth would be their main base. The new Invincible-class aircraft carriers were also to be based in Portsmouth. Amid the refit work a number of small oil and tank-cleaning lighters were built and launched in great style.

The Cod Wars brought unexpected work to the dockyard in the form of collision damage. The Royal Navy's lightly built frigates were no match for the robustly built Icelandic gunboats.

The decade ended with news that HMS *Hermes* would be starting a refit to convert her into a ski-ramp aircraft carrier. Over the last ten years the number of dry-dockings had fallen as a consequence of a smaller workforce and navy. In that period 1,042 vessels of all types had been dry-docked or slipped in the dockyard, peaking in 1971 when

Looking south along Main Road from the head of No. 4 Dock (1772). No. 27 Storehouse (1894), with its platform for loading and unloading from railway wagons, is on the left. Behind this building was the Dockyard Surgery (1902), known to dockyard men as the 'Poultice Walloper's Shop'. The large building in the middle ground is No. 24 Store, originally built as four separate storehouses in 1782. Later an additional floor was added and it became home to the MED Drawing Office. In the far distance can be seen the east wing of South Office Block, built in 1788 as a store. The west wing was built as offices in 1786. The two buildings were joined together in the early 1840s by the centre structure.

139 vessels were dry-docked. But by 1979 the number had fallen to fifty-eight. The question had already been asked whether the large number of dry docks could now be justified. To many the answer was known before it was asked.

Many men felt the old dockyard was slipping away from them. Familiar buildings and locations were now unrecognisable in the yard they had grown up with. The managerial side saw many subtle changes. Titles such as Chargemen and Time and Work Recorders became Technical Supervisors and Technical Officers, Finance, in 1969, and Inspectors and Foremen of Crafts also underwent title changes. The time-honoured departments of the dockyard, MCD, MED and EEM, started to give way in 1967 to what was called Functionalisation. Work centres and well-known departments were broken up, often with the pieces reappearing under a seemingly meaningless title of abbreviated words. Modernisation of the yard was essential but needed explaining in a very basic way. The result was a loss of identity for the worker. Many complained there were too many changes too often, but changes there had to be in order for the evolving new facility to meet the navy of the future.

Overlooking No. 2 Basin. The coastal minesweeper *Burnaston* and dockyard tug *Samson* are moored to the wall along Boiler Road. The long building is the old Steam Factory (1848). The cranes to No. 5 Slipway and No. 3 Ship Shop (1844) are to the right. No. 2 Slipway can be seen in the middle ground. No. 1 Slipway can be seen by the bucket dredger. The large building just above the Steam Factory to the left is the Old Steam Smithery (1852).

Removing some of the old caisson-hauling machinery from the locks. The pneumatic sliding caissons were installed during the 1870s. This machinery was positioned at the end of a camber let into the side of the lock and connected to the caisson by two endless chains. By tensioning one or the other side of the chain the caisson could be hauled in or out.

There were fifteen dry docks and four locks in the dockyard, all connected to three main pumping stations by a system of underground culverts. It was another world of the dockyard that most who worked there did not see or hear about. This picture was taken during a survey of the culverts in 1978.

A high-tech navy still requires some old traditional skills. Riggers in the Rigging Shop making a collision mat.

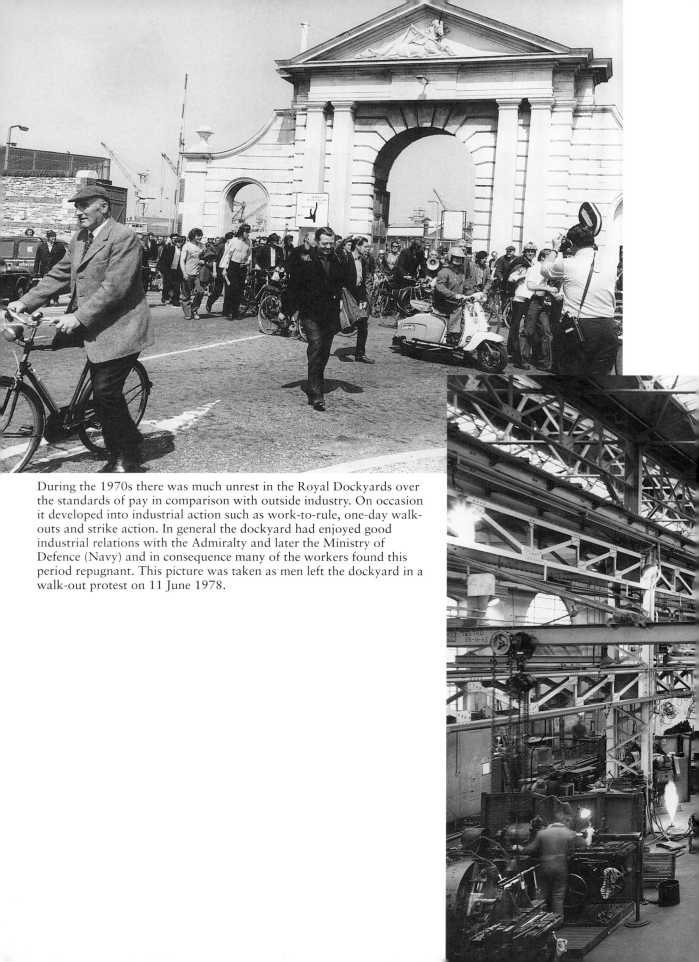

During the 1970s there was much unrest in the Royal Dockyards over the standards of pay in comparison with outside industry. On occasion it developed into industrial action such as work-to-rule, one-day walk-outs and strike action. In general the dockyard had enjoyed good industrial relations with the Admiralty and later the Ministry of Defence (Navy) and in consequence many of the workers found this period repugnant. This picture was taken as men left the dockyard in a walk-out protest on 11 June 1978.

Following spread: A 1975 view across the western side of the dockyard from the top of the old 240-ton crane. The ship nearest the wall is the destroyer *Matapan*, converted to a sonar trials ship. F36 is HMS *Whitby* and F84 is HMS *Exmouth*. The MED Factory (1904) can be seen in the upper right corner and the square white building slightly to the left of centre is the new Amalgamated Pipe Shop, opened in June 1974. The building with three apexes behind it is the Coppersmith Shop (1929).

The Coppersmith Shop in the late 1970s, built by the Navy Works Department in 1928–9 at a cost of £32,000, with machinery costing an additional £12,000. When opened in 1929 it employed over 200 men and boasted of being the best-equipped workshop of its type in the country.

Looking south from No. 13 Dock on 13 June 1972. Note the Second World War air-raid shelter at the head of the dock. The large building on the left is the old boilermakers' shop. Stretching over to the right are the sawmills and the open wood store, and out of sight behind that is the old saw-sharpening shop. The building on the right with the chimneys is the Foreman of the Yard's office. (Only shipwright foremen were known as Foremen of the Yard.) It was always referred to as 'the Bungalow' but no one ever seemed to know why.

In a view of 3 February 1972, No. 3 Ship Shop (1844) is on the left. Its 80ft-high roof was supported on graceful arches which became the model for architects of many of the large railway stations in later years. HMS *Eagle* is on the jetty behind, de-equipping. To the right is the Prefabricating Welding Shop. The other building slightly to the right is No. 3 Smithery. The cranes to the slipway were finally demolished in October 1977 as a start in the development of the North Corner Group. The slipway is surrounded with the usual clutter of toolbox sheds, lay-apart stores and welding grids.

CHAPTER 10

THE FALKLANDS TO THE GULF, 1980–90

'People working in the Royal Dockyards are an integral part of the Navy and it is inconceivable that closure of Portsmouth Dockyard should even be seriously contemplated.' These were the words of the First Sea Lord, Admiral Sir Henry Leach, after a day touring the yard talking to managers and workers. It was 1980 and no one in the dockyard really doubted his words. But morale slowly slipped away as the pay in the Royal Dockyards continually fell below that of outside industry, which was a steady drain on the manpower of the yard. The Navy Minister, Mr Keith Speed, stated on a fact-finding tour of the yard in November 1979 that the pay and the finance structure must be adjusted if the loss of skilled labour was to be stopped.

Part of the Chief Executive of the dockyard's annual report for 1979–80 was reproduced in the dockyard's local paper, *Trident*, in July 1980. It made sombre reading for the yardmen. It showed that Devonport Dockyard had a larger workforce than Portsmouth and a larger slice of the ship repair work. The crown of the principal dockyard was slowly slipping away from Portsmouth. In September 1980 the Navy Minister said,

'Although the government has published a Consultative Document on the future of the four home Royal Dockyards, it should not be assumed that final decisions have been taken.' At the same time it was reported that the Chief of Fleet Support, Vice Admiral Sir William Pillar, stressed the need for four home Royal Dockyards. Also in the report he went on to say, 'Personally I will be sad to see the special relationship which has existed between the Royal Navy and the Dockyards replaced by a commercial one based on a trading fund, but it is quite obvious that something must be done.'

During this period the need for Portsmouth Dockyard was often seen in the press, and praise was heaped on the dockyard by prominent parties. Often the old dockyard saying was heard quoted by men of the yard at this time: 'Beware of pats on the back; they're only feeling for a soft place to put in the knife.' Who could blame them for thinking it, for they had heard it all before?

Only a few months later, in 1981, John Nott was appointed Secretary of State for Defence with the task of rationalising defence policy and spending. He took a stronger line in the support of NATO, in which the Army and Royal Air Force were already firmly committed. The axe fell upon the Royal Navy and its supporting services. Keith Speed resigned from the post of Navy Minister in May, presumably in protest at the things he saw for the future.

When the Secretary of State for Defence made his announcement in Parliament on 25 June 1981 it came as a shattering blow to the Royal Navy and its people. It was to be reduced to two carriers, and the amphibious landing vessels phased out. The number of destroyers and frigates was to be reduced from fifty-nine to fifty. The Royal Fleet Auxiliary and the Royal Maritime Auxiliary Services were also to be cut. Chatham and Pembroke Dockyards were to be closed. Portsmouth was to be reduced to a naval base, with no refitting capability. Gibraltar Dockyard was also to be reduced. The closure of naval stores depots and oil fuel depots over the country included Deptford, Invergordon, Llangennech, Pembroke Dock and Woolston. Some 16,000 jobs would be lost, with the first redundancies being issued within the year. For Portsmouth it meant that the General Manager's Department would be reduced from the present 4,750 to 1,000 and with proportional cuts in the Captain of the Port's Department, Finance, Personnel, Transport and Naval Stores Departments. Altogether it was estimated that between 6,000 and 7,000 jobs would be lost in the dockyard as a whole. A Job Centre was to be set up in the dockyard.

On 7 July thousands of dockyard men and women travelled to London by special train, coach and car to join with colleagues from Chatham Dockyard in a mass lobby of Parliament while the House debated the planned defence cuts. It was to no avail. The outlook for Portsmouth as a city was indeed bleak, with many thousands of its citizens feeling betrayed by a government to which they had given their cherished vote.

The Secretary of State for Defence, Mr John Nott, made what some referred to as an ill-advised visit to Portsmouth on 9 September and tried to address a crowd of up to 2,000 dockyard employees outside the Central Office Block 1. His visit was in response to a promise he had made to the yard's trade unions at national level after his announcement of the dockyard's run-down. It was to be a low-key visit with a tour of the yard in a minibus. However, when it became known that he was in the dockyard a crowd started to gather. The Port Admiral, Rear Admiral Tippet, believed he had an assurance that if the Secretary of State agreed to talk to the crowd he would be given a hearing.

On emerging from the glass-fronted entrance Mr Nott was booed and jeered and met with a barrage of hammers, iron bolts, tomatoes and eggs as he tried to speak. During the mêlée the plate-glass panels to the entrance and glass panels in the revolving door were broken. The Ministry of Defence later issued a statement denying that the Secretary of State had been hit, but the Port Admiral, who was in his party, had been kicked. Eventually the Minister was smuggled out of the back of the building (it was said, disguised as a policeman) and into the coach. Another small crowd was waiting and further missiles were thrown as the coach pulled away.

It was an unpleasant incident but demonstrated the helpless feeling of the dockyard men. It came in the same week that 178 apprentices who had finished their time left the yard as there were no jobs for them, and for the majority of the dockyard workforce it seemed there was no hope for the future.

It's war! The crowds wrap up their flags and disperse as the *Hermes* and *Invincible* disappear in the mist. Only the loved ones linger on, wondering. The words of Rudyard Kipling were as true then as when written at the turn of the century:

When you've shouted 'Rule Britannia', when you've sung 'God Save the Queen',
When you've finished killing Kruger with your mouth,
Will you kindly drop a shilling in my little tambourine
For a gentleman in *kharki* ordered South?
He's an absent-minded beggar and his weaknesses are great –
But we and Paul must take him as we find him –
He is out on active service, wiping something off a slate –
And he's left a lot of little things behind him!
Duke's son – cook's son – son of a hundred kings –
(Fifty thousand horse and foot going to Table Bay!)
Each of 'em doing his country's work
(and who's to look after their things?)
Pass the hat for your credit's sake,
And pay – pay – pay!

At 2.45 on the morning of Friday 2 April 1982, while the people of Portsmouth slept, the Prime Minister received a message informing her of Argentina's impending invasion of the Falkland Islands. At 3.30 the first signal was issued to bring the Fleet in home ports to short notice for sea. For the dockyard men, Friday was the day appointed when they would report to their heads of line management and collect their formal notices of redundancy. By 10.30 most had received them and had either screwed them up in disgust or quietly slipped them into their pockets. At 11.00 the news broke in the yard: 'We're sending the Fleet south, and they're leaving Monday morning.' Within an hour the dockyard turned from a place of gloom and despondency to a humming beehive of activity.

The *Invincible* was in the yard, having operational defects put right, and most of her crew were on Easter leave. *Hermes* was in the second week of her Dockyard Assisted Maintenance Period, with her superstructure hidden by scaffolding and much of her machinery under refit. *Intrepid* had paid off and was being de-stored, with the possibility of an impending sale. The stores ship *Stromness*, which was to play a major part in the campaign, had been decommissioned and put up for sale.

The flight deck of *Hermes* was cleared and the scaffolding dismantled with breathtaking speed as the first of eight Harrier aircraft was flown in during the afternoon. On Saturday, Sea King helicopters flew onto *Hermes* and *Invincible*, and on Sunday eleven more Harriers flew in to join the two carriers. The Herculean task of storing the ships for war in hostile and distant waters soon became evident as thousands of tons of stores, oil, ammunition and equipment began to arrive by helicopter, road, rail and sea.

The Oiling Department at Gosport worked tirelessly, bringing thousands of tons of fuel to the waiting ships, as did the Armaments Department at Bedenham, which transported ordnance of all natures in quantities not seen since the Second World War. Every spare man was pressed into service to assist in storing ships as the mountains of stores on the dockside grew. Union representatives turned a blind eye to demarcation as men from all departments responded to the order, 'Ships must sail by Monday morning!'

Never before had the world watched a fleet prepare and leave for war, as it did

The P&O North Sea ferry *Norland* in C Lock on 23 April 1982, being fitted out for the Falklands conflict. Over the space of one weekend she had two helicopter landing pads, water desalination plant, refuelling at sea arrangements, satellite navigation equipment, accommodation for troops and battery-charging facilities fitted, as well as some of her machinery defects rectified. The work was further complicated by the need to store the ship for the voyage. The picture was taken on the Sunday morning, the day before she sailed with 800 men of 2 Para. (2nd Battalion, Parachute Regt).

on that Monday morning. Three days after the order to sail arrived in Portsmouth Dockyard and under the full glare of television, the world watched as the Fleet cleared the mouth of Portsmouth Harbour, passing the Round Tower, which for centuries had seen other great fleets and ships pass on similar duties to do business in deep waters and keep the Monarch's peace. How ironic it seemed for a fleet to be dispatched to fight a war in distant waters without allies, at a time when politicians were declaring that the defence review had been brought about partly because Britain would never be called on to fight a war on its own again.

From April to July forty-four warships and merchant ships were modified or repaired as a result of Operation Corporate, the code name for the Falklands campaign, in addition to the normal workload of the yard. The response from the men who had just been issued with their redundancy notices has been described many times as magnificent, but behind it all was a hope that there would be a reappraisal of the defence strategy.

By July, ships of the Fleet were returning to their home ports. Portsmouth was to see many such joyful and spectacular events. They were made more enjoyable following the announcement in June that no more redundancy notices would be issued and that the planned run-down would be put on hold. Commercial ships employed during Operation Corporate were known as STUFT ships (Ships Taken Up From Trade). Eighteen such vessels were modified in the dockyard and by September the job comically known as 'de-stufting' was under way. This entailed de-equipping and returning the ships to their owners.

An announcement in the House of Commons in December brought some Christmas cheer to city and dockyard when it was stated that the planned workforce of the dockyard would be enlarged to 2,800 as a result of the retention of additional warships in the Fleet and the need to update weapons systems in the light of the Falklands War. Redundant buildings in the yard would be taken over by the Naval Stores Department to house additional stores from the closure of other establishments in the country. Ship refits would also be undertaken. The dockyard of the future would be known as the Fleet Maintenance and Repair Organisation, or FMRO. Old yardmen jokingly called themselves 'frimroses', but it would take a long time (if at all) for the term 'dockyard' to disappear or the more endearing term 'dockyard matey'. This is said to go back to the time of the Napoleonic Wars and press-gangs, when dockyard employees were issued with a brass exception tag on which was stamped 'His Majesty's Dockyard man' (or 'people'; the wording was said to vary from time to time). The word 'Majesty', was often abbreviated as 'Maties' or 'Matey', and the term 'dockyard maties' or 'matey' was born.

On 1 October 1984 a notice in *The Times* 'Obituaries' column announced: 'HM Dockyard at Portsmouth passed peacefully away at midnight on 30th September after many years faithful service, and will be sadly missed.' The originator has remained a mystery, but it was a sentiment felt by many thousands of people. On 1 October the dockyard became FMRO, a department under the overall umbrella of Portsmouth Naval Base.

In April 1985 a start was made at demolishing the 240-ton hammer-head crane that dominated the skyline not only of the dockyard but also of Portsmouth.

On coming over Portsdown Hill and into Portsmouth, people often remarked it was the first thing to catch their eye. It was built in 1912 and was in fact a 250-ton crane, but for some unexplained reason it was always referred to as the 240-tonner. Structurally it was quite sound but it was said to be surplus to future requirements. Sadly, it was gone by August. Glasgow had a similar crane, which has now been preserved for posterity.

Another old friend to leave the dockyard was the Admiralty Floating Dock at the north end of the yard. AFD 26 came to Portsmouth in 1959 from Portland. Her first dry-docking at Portsmouth was the submarine *Trespasser* on 15 June 1959, her last being the submarine *Otus* on 10 October 1986. During her service in the dockyard she had dry-docked 400 submarines and seventeen other vessels. She was towed first to Blundell & Crompton Ltd at Tilbury Docks for a sixteen-week refit, and then to Rosyth to be used primarily for conventional-submarine dry-dockings.

Between 1983 and 1986 the new organisation ran into many teething troubles, especially with the reduction in manpower, relocation of plant and the birth pains of a new management system. It was not unnatural to expect a loss of cohesion within the organisation and for a time the operation of quality-management systems, necessary to satisfy the requirements of Defence Standard 05-21, the MOD(N) standard accreditation certificate, became more

HMS *Hermes* comes through the harbour mouth to a hero's welcome on 21 July 1982. Her rust-stained hull said much for the terrible conditions experienced in those cold, hostile seas. Since leaving Portsmouth on 5 April she had spent 108 days continually at sea, travelling over 35,000 miles.

A tremendous welcome awaited HMS *Fearless* and *Intrepid* on 14 July 1982 as they berthed at Fountain Lake Jetty in the dockyard. Families, friends and dockyard men greeted the two grand old ladies as helicopters flew overhead in salute. A rethink on the defence policy had spared both ships for the foreseeable future.

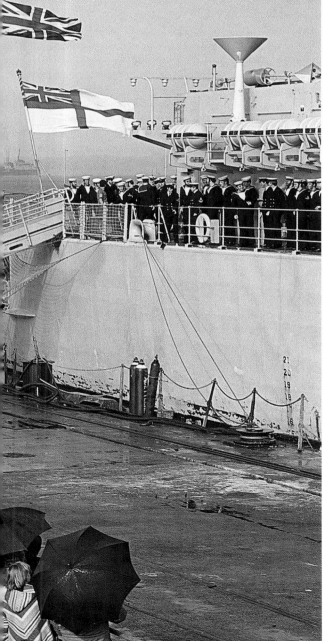

Home from the sea. HMS *Southampton* and *Birmingham* berthing at Fountain Lake Jetty in 1983 as families keenly wait for the moment to board and see their loved ones. HMS *Diomede* is astern of *Birmingham*, concluding a refit.

HMS *Invincible* and HMS *Bristol* come home to a tumultuous welcome on 17 September 1982. The splendour of the occasion was endorsed by the presence of HM the Queen and the Duke of Edinburgh, who had come to welcome their son Prince Andrew home. He had served as a helicopter pilot in *Invincible*.

difficult to maintain. But by April 1987 FMRO could once more boast that they had achieved the necessary accreditation to MOD(N) and NATO standards.

In 1987 also occurred the first dry-docking of a nuclear submarine in Portsmouth. HMS/m *Swiftsure* was dry-docked in C Lock from Friday 9 until Saturday 10 October. The western end of C Lock had been specially adapted for the use of nuclear submarines.

On 21 January 1989 the last under-water dive by a dockyard diver using the standard diving dress was made into the waters of No. 10 Dry Dock at the undocking of the submarine *Onyx*. Mr Eric Walker, the supervisor of the diving team, donned the helmet for the last time. It was 151 years after Auguste

Siebe invented the standard diving dress that the era of the helmeted diver ended. It was replaced by modern diving equipment.

On 16 March 1989 another milestone was reached when the RMAS tender *Froxfield* became the 200th vessel to be dry-docked by FMRO since vesting day on 1 October 1984. A breakdown of the numbers showed that dockings comprised 8 aircraft carriers, 37 destroyers, 16 frigates, 63 submarines, 16 minehunter/sweepers, 7 support ships, 10 landing craft, 39 RMAS craft and 6 caissons. The numbers show that although the old dockyard now had a new name and had shrunk in size and manpower, the old spirit of 'can do' still prevailed and was ready to meet any new challenge.

The tractor tug *Fiona* and Armaments Lighter 329(A) in No. 10 Dock. No. 7 Dock was built along with the Steam Basin (No. 2 Basin) and opened by Queen Victoria in 1848. In 1858 No. 10 Dock was built on to the end of No. 7 Dock and opened on to the harbour. The two docks were joined by a caisson which, when removed, made one long dock, at that time known as the continuation dock. This was the only dry dock in Portsmouth that could dry-dock the *Warrior* until the completion of No. 11 Dock in 1865. The connecting caisson was replaced by a concrete roadway and wall in the 1920s. No. 7 Dock was filled in in 1989 and No. 10 Dock in 1991.

An aerial view overlooking the Camber at Old Portsmouth, HMS *Vernon* (now Gunwharf Quays), the Harbour station and the western half of the dockyard. In the top left-hand corner of the picture is HMS *Tiger*, with HMS *Hermes* alongside King's Stairs Jetty. The merchant ship at South Railway Jetty is thought to be the *Avelonia Star*. The picture is dated 1984.

Above: After the Falklands War, lessons learnt were slowly adopted into the Fleet. One consequence was the removal of ships' motorboats and their davits in favour of additional anti-aircraft armament. The picture shows No. 4 Boathouse during the early 1980s. The increasing use of inflatable craft saw a rapid decline in the boat-repair facilities of the dockyard.

Right: Unseen and unsung is the work of those employed in the bottom of docks. The Slinging Party and fitters remove the port after stabiliser from HMS *Invincible* in D Lock.

CHAPTER 11

TOWARDS THE NEW MILLENNIUM, 1990–2000

The last decade of the century brought more of the changes and fears for the future that had become almost commonplace in defence establishments during the 1980s. Discussions on the future viability of the FMRO organisation were ongoing. In February 1990 it was announced that the old Dockyard Cost and Management Accounting System (DCMA) was giving way to a new organisation known as MAFIS: Management Accounting and Finance Information System.

In May of that year the Portsmouth Dockyard local newspaper, *Trident*, proudly announced on the front page: 'MAFIS goes live'. Also on the front page was a heading which said that FMRO was declaring its new aims. There followed a description of the new management system, with department heads whose departments were abbreviated to initial capitals, which left readers in the lower order of the organisation none the wiser. Underneath this heading, and printed in red, was: 'FMRO RETAINS AQAP1 STATUS'. Although this was in itself a credible achievement, for the man on the

job with the spanner in his hand it must have been a bewildering statement. But it was one that seemed to fit well with an era when qualifications and departments were reduced to abbreviations that often only those in the department concerned could interpret.

May also saw the closure of the Royal Naval Armament Depot at Priddy's Hard, ending over 250 years of service, first to the Board of Ordnance and then to the Royal Navy. Originally the land had been purchased by the Ordnance Department in 1759 from the Vicar of Fareham, Thomas Missing, and Jane Priddy for the building of fortifications. At that time gunpowder for the garrison and the Fleet was still housed in the Square Tower at Old Portsmouth and did not move to Priddy's Hard until later, in 1771, when the powder magazine was completed. In 1994, 25 acres of the site, including the old powder magazine, were offered to Gosport Borough Council and this land is now home to Explosion, the Museum of Naval Firepower.

On 19 May 1991 FMRO held a families' day, when over 2,000 employees and their families were able to enjoy a range of exhibitions and demonstrations, reflecting the wide-ranging skills and activities encompassed within the FMRO organisation in support of the Fleet. The centre of activities was the small area at the head of No. 13 Dry Dock, where a funfair atmosphere prevailed, with sideshows and the opportunity to throw water bags at senior managers who put their heads through a cut-out sailor. There were diving and mobile-crane displays, with no shortage of children wanting to take the controls. All the major workshops, including the Central Boiler House and Main Pump House, responded well to the event, throwing open their doors for viewing and demonstrations. HMS *Nottingham*, the yard's main project at the time, was also open to viewing, as was HMS *Gloucester*, which had recently returned from the Gulf. The event finished with a Grand Draw, which raised over £1,500 for St Mary's Hospital. Mrs Jean Crump, wife of Constructor Captain John Crump,

Director, Maintenance and Repair, performed the draw.

When the event was first announced it received little interest from the general workforce, but as it progressed so it generated enthusiasm and in the end restored much of the lost pride of the workforce in the skills, activities and plant of the new Fleet Maintenance and Repair Organisation. For many it was the first time that their families and friends actually saw the environment in which they worked, what they did and the high degree of skill they possessed to carry it out. Even the most cynical had to admit it had been a tremendous morale-booster. On 20 June 1993 FMRO held its third and most successful families' day, with over 4,500 visitors attending and raising over £3,500 for the Portsmouth Hospital Appeal.

Another milestone in the history of the organisation was reached when in accordance with government policy of putting dockyards and bases under commercial management control, the

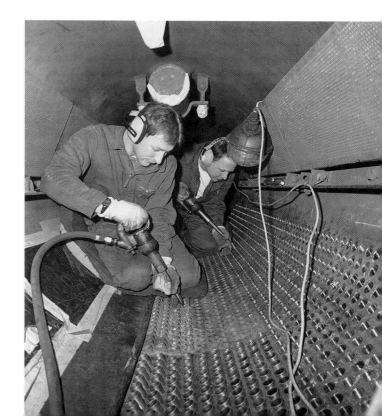

The home base of the Royal Yacht *Britannia* was at Portsmouth and the dockyard took great pride in her finished appearance. During February 1992 the *Britannia* was in the Naval Base for a refit. The picture shows the confined conditions in which boilermakers work when retubing one of her boilers.

Fleet Maintenance and Repair Organisation was taken over by Fleet Support Limited (FSL). The company, formed by BAE Systems and Vosper Thornycroft to manage the FMRO, formally took over following vesting day on 28 February 1998.

In August 1993 another slice of the old dockyard disappeared when it was announced that the small-craft refitting section of the Round Tower Complex would no longer refit small craft but would become a garage service. The director of the complex, Commander Malcolm Farrow, suggested that the completion of the last wooden-hull harbour launch refitted at the complex should be marked by a social event and so it was that the youngest lady on the staff, a Miss Sara Malthouse, broke a bottle of champagne on the bows of Harbour Launch 6507 before the vessel was slipped into the waters of the harbour. Since the complex had opened in 1976 there had been just over 300 harbour launch refits as well as 630 GRP craft and 525 steel-boat refits. Because of the size of these vessels, they are not recorded in the main Docking Register of the yard. The number of unprogrammed jobs accepted often averaged 800 per quarter, which stands as a credit to the professionalism of all who worked in this small and often overlooked section of the old dockyard.

In 1985 a heritage area had been established in the old part of the dockyard running from the Main Gate (now known as Victory Gate) to HMS *Victory* and encompassing the three Georgian storehouses and the Victorian boathouses flanking the tourist route to HMS *Victory*. The Royal Naval Museum, the *Mary Rose* and HMS *Warrior* 1860 were also included in the heritage area. In 1986 the Portsmouth Naval Base Property Trust was set up to take on a lease from the MOD of the heritage area, which now became known as Portsmouth Historic Dockyard, and find new uses for the historic buildings that would safeguard their future and attract more visitors to the area.

In November 1993 the Property Trust announced plans to spend over £2 million on three projects in the Historic Dockyard. A new visitors' centre was planned to cater for the growing numbers of tourists, now approaching 500,000 a year, and the Porter's Lodge (1708) would be refurbished and converted to offices for the Flagship Portsmouth Trust, which was responsible for marketing and ticketing the Historic Dockyard attractions. In addition, the wooden No. 7 Boathouse on the north side of the old Mast Pond (1665) also came in for attention. This boathouse, built in 1801, had been dismantled and then reassembled in 1875, when new cast-iron piles replaced the original wooden ones on which it stood over the Mast Pond. The new project involved replacing the old corrugated-iron roof with a slate roof, and refitting the interior with a 350-seat restaurant, a themed gift shop and the Dockyard Apprentice exhibition, showing the skills of a dockyard apprentice in 1910. The artefacts for this display were drawn from the collection of the Portsmouth Royal Dockyard Historical Trust. There was also an education area for the increasing numbers of school parties that now found naval and dockyard industrial history part of the national curriculum.

The Property Trust had already invested considerable sums in restoring the outer fabric of the three Georgian storehouses and rebuilding the elegant clock tower of No. 10 Storehouse, which had been

One of the attractions at the FMRO Families' Day was a large water tank where the Diving Section demonstrated their skills for the public, watched through large, armoured windows. Here a little girl enjoys playing a game of noughts and crosses with the diver in the tank.

destroyed by German bombing in the Second World War. This clock had marked time for countless thousands of sailors and dockyard men for over 170 years and it was a most welcome rebirth and a credit to the Property Trust for its execution.

On 25 March 1994 the new Victory Building was opened. This was to be the headquarters of the Second Sea Lord and his staff, who had been moved from London and integrated with CINCNAVHOME at Portsmouth. The site had previously been occupied by the Joiners' Shop, the Dockyard Photographic Unit and the Medical Centre, or as the yardmen called it, the 'Poultice Walloper's Shop'. Also on the site was the Mould Loft

Floor from which all the great battleships, cruisers and modern frigates had been laid out in a plan form, allowing wooden moulds to be made of plates, frames and longitudinals, etc. before erection on the slipway. In its time it had been one of the most important buildings of the dockyard. All this was part of the programme that became known as 'Options for Change' and saw the grouping of many other naval departments, including the Commandant General of Royal Marines, into the Portsmouth area, undeniably demonstrating the continued importance of Portsmouth to the Royal Navy.

The ice patrol ship HMS *Endurance* in C Lock on 28 September 1992, refitting for her return to the southern seas and Antarctica.

Work in the yard continued with its normal run of refits or overhauls of one sort or another but the tempo had changed. Many dry docks now lay empty, partly because of a much smaller Fleet and also a much smaller workforce and facilities. The number of dry-dockings in the yard in the first half of the decade showed a marked contrast compared with the equivalent period in the previous decade.

1990..........27 vessels
1991..........37 vessels
1992..........22 vessels
1993..........39 vessels
1994..........25 vessels
1995..........36 vessels

In 1998 the Naval Base hosted IFOS, the International Festival of the Sea. It was the biggest and most spectacular maritime event ever staged, with 23 Royal Navy ships participating, together with warships from Belgium, Germany, Turkey and France, 30 tall ships and 700 smaller vessels of all shapes and sizes. Over the four days of the festival, more than 200,000 people poured through the old dockyard gates into the Naval Base. Ironically, to the general public and foreign visitors it was still the dockyard.

As the new millennium approached it was announced that a new class of destroyer, the Type 45, was to be built to replace the ageing Type 42s. The shipbuilders Vosper Thornycroft were to be one of the lead players in the new programme. On 18 February 2002 Vosper Thornycroft signed a contract with the prime contractor, BAE Systems, for work on the first six Type 45 warships. Five days later Martin Jay, Chief Executive of Vosper Thornycroft, and John Coles, Chief Executive of Warship Support, signed an agreement that opened the way for the company to begin a 125-year lease of a substantial part of the Naval Base, initially for building sections of the new Type 45 destroyers. After an absence of thirty or more years, shipbuilding would return to Portsmouth. In the summer of 2002 Portsmouth received another boost when it was announced that the two new planned aircraft carriers, each with a displacement of 60,000 tons, would be based at Portsmouth and that Vosper Thornycroft would be hoping to construct sections of these ships in their new multi-million-pound complex now being built in the south-eastern corner of No. 3 Basin. And so another doorway in the long history of the old Royal Dockyard at Portsmouth was opening.

How strange that on 2 October 1905 the revolutionary battleship *Dreadnought* was laid down in Portsmouth Dockyard at a time that marked a turning point for the Royal Navy and the dockyard, and now almost 100 years later the Royal Navy and Portsmouth were at another such turning point. Much had happened in that 100 years. Ships and technology had changed almost beyond comprehension but the men were still the same and the 'can do' attitude still prevailed in the service and civilian workforce.

The relationship between naval personnel and the dockyard workforce had always been a strange marriage. Their criticisms of each other were in the main unjustified and for the most part in good humour. The dockyard matey considered he had every right to criticise and run down the navy and its personnel; after all, it was his navy. But woe betide anyone from outside the yard who criticised the navy. Invariably the matey would leap to their defence like a terrier. When a ship came back to her home port there would be familiar and friendly faces at both ends

The River-class minesweeper HMS *Orwell* in No. 15 Dock in May 1996, having a foul-weather tent erected around her. Not so many years ago this would have been unthinkable; extreme cold and wet clothing were familiar to all who worked on ships in the dockyard. Advances in modern materials and construction methods made this innovation possible. *Orwell*, renamed *Essequibo*, was transferred to the Guyana Coastguard in 2001.

of the gangway, with good humoured banter such as 'We ain't got you lot again, have we?', to be answered with 'Gone and broke yer boat again, have yer?' This attitude was not the prerogative of Portsmouth Dockyard alone, for each of the Royal Dockyards considered that they were the best. In reality each had their strengths and weaknesses, which in the end levelled themselves out.

Many of the friends and relatives of dockyard workers probably considered they had an easy time at work, for invariably on returning home they would not talk of their job in the yard. How could they, for they lived in a world that was totally alien to most of the people in the town and country? But they did talk of Joe the bookie's runner, Ginger who was always doing a rabbit job, Chalky who constantly made tea, or old Thunder-boots who was always mending his bike, which helped sustain the idea that little work was done. But the sheer volume of work that annually flowed through the dockyard and its outstations belied any criticism of slackness of the dockyard worker.

Many of the young apprentices of the 1940s and 50s period were now the old men of the yard and still talked of the battleships, armoured fleet carriers and heavy cruisers of their youth. The majority of them would be contemplating leaving the yard within a few years. Many had said they were not leaving the yard, it had already left them, and how true this was, for it had changed almost beyond recognition in its organisation, management and physical appearance. The young people of the workforce tended to accept the changes more readily for they had not seen the dockyard as it had been in former years and consequently had no yardstick to measure it by except for the tales of the older men, which were often biased to

their particular way of thinking. But they would also be old men one day and they also would bemoan the modern establishment and talk of the great ships of their youth. It is the way of things. The changing nature of warship design had always been part of the dockyard ethos and every new class of warship brought forth new technologies in weapons, propulsion, communication, detection and construction, which the dockyard had always greedily absorbed.

But changes over the last few years had been like nothing they had experienced before. Most were convinced that politicians did not understand or care for the importance of a well-balanced navy and its support services, and they smiled at the enthusiasm of some senior officers who would proclaim after each defence cut, 'We have the balance right now. We are leaner and meaner,' and suspected that they were, in the best traditions of the service, making the best of a bad job.

How can one measure the success or failure of an industry such as the dockyard? It is hard to judge. On occasions criticism fell on poor management, which in the main was unjust, for they managed a workforce and plant that were invariably underfunded by a system that was always imposed upon them. There have been occasions when, in time of dire need, the country could not have done without Portsmouth Dockyard. It is easy after the event to say that if it had not been there they would have found somewhere else, but history has shown that it is its geographical location which on such occasions gives it its importance. In those times of crisis the response to unplanned and unprogrammed work has been a great credit to the flexibility, skill and determination of all who worked in the dockyard.

The Type 23 (Duke-class) frigate HMS *Lancaster* has just docked down in No. 15 Dock on 16 May 1996. Shipwrights and slingers are waiting for the last of the water to be drained away so that they can erect additional timber shoring under the bilges and at the after-end cut-up. When the ship touches the blocks in the dry-docking operation she is said to have 'sewed'. It comes from the old Anglo-Saxon word for drain, sharing its derivation with the word 'sewer'.

HMS *Fearless* in C Lock with her brood of chicks in July 1996. In the 1920s, when the battleships *Nelson* and *Rodney* came to Portsmouth, the lower midship areas of the lower alters (steps) had to be cut away so that they could just sit down in the dock. Today it is the only reminder we have of their great size.

In the final analysis it is the quality and quantity of the product produced by an industry that marks its success. The quality speaks for itself. The customer would not have returned if he had not been satisfied. As for the quantity, well, from June 1936 until 1 October 1984 when the old dockyard gave way to FMRO, they had slipped or dry-docked over 9,796 vessels; from October 1984 to December 1995 the new organisation had dry-docked 445 vessels: a total of 10,241.

(It would not be surprising to find that for the whole century this figure is nearer 19,000.) These dry-dockings ranged from the great battleships to the humble little lighter. The figure excludes the countless thousands of vessels that, over that same period of time, were not dry-docked, but still had substantial work carried out on them. Not a bad little epitaph for an industry where the local population would joke, 'How many work in the dockyard? Well, only about half of them.'

Opposite: This September 1996 view shows the EOB (East Office Block), now the headquarters of FMRO (Fleet Maintenance and Repair Organisation), the refit organisation of the Naval Base. The Type 42 (Batch 3) destroyer HMS *Manchester* is in No. 14 Dock. HMS *Ark Royal* can be seen laid up in No. 3 Basin in the background with HMS *Intrepid*.

Without doubt one of the most joyous occasions in the dockyard was the International Festival of the Sea from 28 to 31 August 1998. Over 200,000 people poured in through the gates to see 23 Royal Navy vessels, naval ships from Belgium, Turkey, Germany and France, 30 tall sailing ships and 700 smaller vessels of different shapes and sizes. The eighteenth-century street market in Anchor Lane was one of the main shore attractions. The picture shows the *Grand Turk*, a replica of an eighteenth-century frigate, moored with other vessels at the North Wall of the Naval Base.

The Wight Link car ferry *St Cecilia* and the passenger ferry *Lady Patricia* in C Lock on 14 January 1997. Not since the 1920s had the dockyard (now FMRO) undertaken commercial shipping work. One of the Invincible-class aircraft carriers can be seen in D Lock.

A 1999 view looking eastwards across the north end of the Naval Base. HMS *Fearless* is in the far distance, followed by two Type 23 frigates, and HMS *Exeter* is being pushed on to the wall by the tugs *Sheepdog* and *Genevieve*, with the tug *Bustler* standing by.

HMS *Bristol* can be seen in the left of this 1999 picture, moored just south of Whale Island. The aircraft carrier is believed to be HMS *Illustrious* and to the right of the picture are two Type 42 destroyers.

A fine aerial picture of No. 3 Basin in 1996. The ship in the bottom left corner is thought to be THV *Patricia*. The guided missile destroyer in the bottom of the picture is probably HMS *Kent*. HMS *Intrepid* is on the south side of the Promontory. On the north side, the inner ship is thought to be either *Rame Head* or *Berry Head*, and the Leander-class frigate HMS *Scylla* is on the outside. HMS *Ark Royal* is laid up on the north inner wall of the basin with the Royal Fleet Auxiliary repair ship *Diligence* outside. HMS *Bristol* is in the top right-hand corner of the picture with a Type 23 frigate just ahead of HMS *Invincible*. In the Pocket are two more Leander-class frigates and two Ton-class coastal minesweepers. The Royal Yacht *Britannia* is in D Lock together with crane lighter No. 4, whose designation, when abbreviated and expressed in Roman numerals, spawned the vessel's nickname – 'Clive'.

A view of the South Wall of Promontory from the 240-ton crane, 25 May 1944. The Captain-class frigate HMS *Dacres* (K472) lies alongside an O-class destroyer being readied for action. A Bangor-class minesweeper and a Flower-class corvette are tied up beyond.

APPENDIX

The work undertaken by the dockyard and surrounding establishments during the D-Day period would itself present a sizeable volume. It is therefore of interest to examine part of the report dated 16 August 1944 from the Admiral Superintendent of Portsmouth Dockyard to the Commander-in-Chief Portsmouth on the involvement of the establishment during the D-Day operation. (National Archives, ADM 179/513) I have summarised the report to highlight the sheer volume of work that flowed through the dockyard during that momentous period.

1. Subsequently and by degrees the dockyard became more and more involved in Operation Overlord. This affected not only the personnel employed directly on ship repair, but also those whose business it was to serve the dockyard and the many shore establishments which, in this Command, extended from Cumberland in the north through the Midlands to Portland in the west and Newhaven in the east.

2. The total numbers of workpeople employed did not vary appreciably throughout the whole period. The numbers borne on managers of constructive, engineering and electrical departments amounted to just over 15,000, of whom 2,300 were women. Between 50 and 60 per cent of these were employed directly on repairs, refits and new construction. The remainder were employed on essential work in the maintenance of the Fleet, such as the upkeep and installation of appliances of all sorts in barracks, schools, armaments depots, air stations, victualling yards and hospitals; the manufacture of torpedo tubes, the conversion and repair of stores and the running and maintenance of the port facilities and dockyard services.

3. From the ship-repair point of view all the professional departments of the dockyard were from the earliest days closely associated with the development of special types of craft and equipment and fittings of all kinds, many of which in their final stages would appear to have played a not unimportant part in the landing operation. [The report goes on to mention fifteen examples of such development. See Chapter 6.]

4. Although the dockyard commitment remained substantially to Fleet repair, as D-Day rapidly approached so the volume of work increased, with a considerable number of last-minute modifications to landing craft and the manufacture of special stores, for example 1,000 sets of hydrographic and beach-marking equipment.

5. The numbers of ships and major craft dealt with by the dockyard over this period (the months before D-Day) for refits, boiler cleaning, defects, changing guns, etc. were as follows:

Battleships, cruisers, destroyers, monitors, fleet minesweepers	88
LSTs	16
LCTs	186
Trawlers, drifters, boom defence vessels	30
Miscellaneous craft	53
Coastal forces craft	53

In addition to the above, twelve destroyers and frigates were fitted with bow chaser guns and twenty-four minesweepers with additional equipment. HMS *Durban*, HMS *Centurion* and HNethMS *Sumatra* were prepared as block-ships and HMS *Despatch* was prepared as a headquarters ship. A considerable amount of work was also involved in fitting out HMS *Largs*, HMS *Hilary* and HMS *Bulolo* as headquarters ships for force commanders.

6. For a few days after D-Day the dockyard was not much involved in the landing operations, being mainly concerned with the supply of stores of all descriptions and the evacuation of casualties returning from the far shore.

7. Four days after D-Day, ships began to return for repairs and by 10 June forty landing craft mechanised (LCM) were in hand for repairs. The peak was reached on 17 June, when fifty-two LCMs were in the dockyard undergoing repairs.

8. During this period, work on the following was undertaken by the dockyard or by local firms under dockyard control:

	In hand	Dry-docked	Completed
Minesweepers and larger vessels	76	15	62
LSTs	44	22	41
LCTs	247	203	197
Trawlers, drifters, etc.	65	16	39
Miscellaneous craft	25	13	24
Coastal forces craft	56	33	55

(Vessels 'dry-docked' are included in vessels 'in hand'. Vessels 'completed' presumably excludes vessels passed on to ship repair facilities outside the command or vessels deemed a constructive total loss.)

Large damage repairs to the following vessels were patched and the vessels removed elsewhere for completion of repairs: HMS *Rattlesnake*, *Wrestler*, *Halstead*, *Persian*, *Kellett*, *Trollope*, *Fury*, *Gothland* and *Apollo*, LST 359, USS *Nelson* and FFS *La Surprise*.

BIBLIOGRAPHY

Burt, R.A. *British Battleships 1919–1939*, London, Arms and Armour Press, 1993

British Naval Documents 1204–1960, Naval Records Society

BRs and Manuals relating to Dockyard Procedure, Portsmouth Royal Dockyard Historical Trust Collection

Dockyard pay and muster records 1900–1970, Portsmouth Royal Dockyard Historical Trust Collection

Dry Docking Register 1936–1979, Portsmouth Royal Dockyard Historical Trust Collection

Evening News (later *The News*), various dates

Goss, J. *Portsmouth Built Warships 1497–1967*, Fareham, Conifer Press, 1984

Hannan, W. *Fifty Years of Naval Tugs*, Liskeard, Maritime Books, 1987

Hill, J.R. *The Oxford Illustrated History of the Royal Navy*, Oxford University Press, 1995

Hough, R. *Dreadnought*, London, Michael Joseph, 1965

Jane's Fighting Ships, London, Sampson Low, Marston & Co., 1900, 1910, 1919, 1934, 1945, 1964, 1976, 1984, 1990

Kemp, P. *British Warship Losses of the 20th Century*, Stroud, Sutton Publishing, 1999

Lenton, H.T. *British and Empire Warships of the Second World War*, London, Greenhill Books, 1989

Manning, T.D. *The British Destroyer*, London, Putnam & Co., 1961

Marriott, L. *Royal Naval Frigates Since 1945*, London, Ian Allan, 1990

Parks, O. *British Battleships*, London, Seeley Service, 1957

Patterson, B.H. *Giv 'er a Cheer Boys. The Great Docks of Portsmouth Dockyard 1830–1914*, Portsmouth, Acme Printing Co., 1989

—— *Ships in and out of Portsmouth*, Portsmouth, Acme Printing Co., 1998

Signals and Loose Documents 1908–1999, Portsmouth Royal Dockyard Historical Trust Collection

Thomas, R.D. and Patterson, B.H. *Dreadnoughts in Camera 1905–1920*, Stroud, Sutton Publishing, 1998

Transactions of the Institute of Naval Architecture, 1918, 1920–1, 1923, 1935–8, 1945, 1947–54

Trident, dockyard newspaper, 1969–95, Portsmouth Royal Dockyard Historical Trust Collection

Whitney, M.J. *Cruisers of the Second World War*, London, Arms and Armour Press, 1996

INDEX

Bold page numbers refer to illustrations.